Coro Jewelry
A COLLECTOR'S GUIDE

*Identification
&
Values*

COLLECTOR BOOKS
A Division of Schroeder Publishing Co., Inc.

Marcia "Sparkles" Brown

❧ Front Cover ❧

Center ✦ Gift box necklace imported from Japan, part of set that includes earrings, $110.00 for set, pg. 162.

Clockwise from left ✦ Silver bird and fountain brooch, $225.00, p. 74; marlin with Lucite belly, $650.00, p. 39; diamenté navette brooch with partially obscured large-faceted green crystal, $350.00, p. 196; double-strand cranberry bead and aurora borealis necklace, $68.00, p. 168; aurora borealis brooch, part of parure that includes necklace and earrings, $655.00 for parure, p. 157; watch with enameled links, $110.00, p. 197.

❧ Back Cover ❧

Center ✦ Blue chaton and rosette necklace, part of parure that includes bracelet and earrings, $235.00 for parure, p. 44.

Clockwise from top right ✦ Sterling vermeil penguin with black enamel body and amber glass belly, $295.00, p. 114; enameled birdcage necklace, part of set that includes earrings, $48.00 for set, p. 158; three-strand bracelet, part of parure that includes necklace and earrings, $295.00 for parure, p. 155; black enamel and diamenté rhinestone Bacchus mask, $695.00, p. 94; Aladdin's Lamp chatelaine with draped chain and tassel, $185.00, p. 113; hoop-skirted woman with moon cabochon face, $205.00, p. 115.

Cover design ✦ Beth Summers   Book design ✦ Erica Weise

Cover photography ✦ Charles R. Lynch

COLLECTOR BOOKS

P.O. Box 3009
Paducah, Kentucky 42002-3009
www.collectorbooks.com

The current values in this book should be used only as a guide. They are not intended to set prices, which vary from one section of the country to another. Auction prices as well as dealer prices vary greatly and are affected by condition as well as demand. Neither the author nor the publisher assumes responsibility for any losses that might be incurred as a result of consulting this guide.

Searching For A Publisher?

We are always looking for people knowledgeable within their fields. If you feel that there is a real need for a book on your collectible subject and have a large comprehensive collection, contact Collector Books.

Contents

Dedication & Acknowledgments

This book is the accumulation of years of research, collecting, and interviews with the Coro alumni. It was born out of my admiration for Coro and the people who made it such a landmark organization. My special thanks and appreciation go to Gene Verri and Jack Feibelman, gentlemen of the finest caliber and devoted to the costume jewelry world. Both men, still involved in Rhode Island jewelry, have been great and dependable sources of information about the early days of Coro. The generous gifts of their time, memories, and documents helped make this book possible.

This book is dedicated to Jack and Gene, and all the former Coro employees — the Coro Jewelry College alumni. Providence Jewelry Museum curator Jane Civens was invaluable in helping me to obtain the old magazine advertisements. Ira Scheck, Colorado jewelry dealer, was kind enough to loan me Coro Duettes for photography.

It takes so many people to make a book that I would be lost without my friends. THANK YOU ALL!

About the Author

This is the fourth book by the author, Marcia "Sparkles" Brown. She is an acknowledged antique and vintage jewelry author, historian, and lecturer, but more important, she is a collector of costume jewelry. Her hobby has become an avocation, providing her with material to host and co-write seven videos in the Hidden Treasure series that won many national awards; books include *Unsigned Beauties of Costume Jewelry*, and two volumes of *Signed Beauties of Costume Jewelry*.

For the past four years she has been the jewelry appraiser for the Calendar Shows and the Palmer Wirf Shows, and she has been with the Medford Southern Oregon Antiques & Collectibles Shows for five years. She serves as the costume jewelry advisor for both the annual *Schroeder's Antiques Price Guide*, and the *Garage Sale & Flea Market Annual*.

For 12 years, she has been a board member of the Southern Oregon Antiques and Collectibles Club. An active member of the International Vintage Fashion and Costume Jewelry Club for ten years, she has contributed many articles to its publication. She spent 12 years developing her skills as an author and as a freelance news reporter for the southern Oregon area and for the Associated Press.

Author's Note

Because of its large production volume, Coro jewelry is easy for the beginning collector to find at an affordable price. It will soon become apparent that the company offered something for every pocketbook, from that of the dime store shopper to that of the society matron.

Your collection can quickly reflect a range from whimsical brooches to both summer and winter styles and to both daytime and evening wear jewelry.

Introduction

GOLDEN PORTALS

Through these golden portals poured the eager students of the Rhinestone Campus. Coro, the unofficial jewelry college of Rhode Island, welcomed all with open arms. Armenian, Romanian, French, German, Italian, American...all nationalities came through the gleaming brass-framed doorway at 167 Point Street in Providence, Rhode Island, to begin their jewelry studies.

Here they could get one-on-one attention from their instructors. They did not have to worry about tuition; to the contrary, here they would earn an hourly wage. Money would go into, not out of, the families' bank accounts.

From these thousands would come the officers of Coro. Stock boys could become salesmen and vice presidents. Students would graduate and become owners of their own jewelry firms. From the thousands of Coro students over the years came jewelry designers, platers, manufacturers, and factory representatives. Marriages between Coro employees would furnish future generations of students.

For the Coro alumni, their time behind the golden portal was the first step towards a sparkling future. Little did they dream of the influence they would have on the generations to come. The city of Providence, the Rhode Island jewelry industry, and the international jewelry market would all be affected by the work of their hearts, brains, and hands.

To this very day, the golden portals can be found still gleaming at 167 Point Street, and the space above the doors still proclaims, "Coro Building." Inside the building, all is changed. Only memories live on.

6

Coro — from the Beginning

CORO HISTORY

In 1901 Emanuel Cohn, a businessman, started the E. Cohn & Company at 508 Broadway in New York City. At that time, there were few department stores that devoted space to a jewelry division, in the Big Apple or anywhere else in the United States. Cohn took his business knowledge and combined it with the jewelry expertise of Carl Rosenberger to create the Cohn and Rosenberger Company in 1903; the two men had a hunch they would be able to develop and corner the undiscovered, virgin territory of the department store.

This was an ingenious plan, an American idea, that was a catalyst to the growth of the American jewelry industry. A legend was in the making, as well as a business that would last for over seventy-five years.

For ten years, the firm produced collar pins, hat pins, sautoirs, beads, and mourning jewelry. It did not manufacture these standard jewelry items; instead, the company assembled findings to produce the final product.

The year 1911 saw many changes in the firm. With the loss of Emanuel Cohn, the founder of the company, plans for the future were affected. A decision had to be made on how to cope with his absence.

The company did not allow the loss of a partner to slow it down. The Cohn family sold its interests to Carl Rosenberger, who took full charge and moved the company forward. The name of Cohn was retained in the memory of this man who also founded the company. The steady growth of business over the past ten years developed the incentive to increase production. Moving down the street to 538 Broadway allowed ample space for the factory in the basement. This facilitated the expansion of the line to include belt buckles, sash pins, and collar supporters.

In 1923, Coro sent buyers to Japan. There the representatives would buy items and send them back to Coro for possible design ideas. Corogram, Incorporated was a division devoted to monograms during a 1926 craze for this style of jewelry. Members of the American public were personalizing everything from pillows to handkerchiefs with their initials. Coro was kept busy making fifty different styles of monograms, many sparkling with rhinestones. Monograms were sold in sets of three, or in singles. The simple alphabet, with letters that could be custom arranged for the individual, helped the overall sales picture for the company well into the year 1932.

The hunch Cohen and Rosenberger had in the beginning paid off; a market had been created, and sales were booming. Now the demand for more inventory necessitated more production and larger factory space. The decision was made to keep the company's New York office in the heart of the jewelry district to attract prospective buyers.

Factory operations were moved to Providence, Rhode Island, where the business occupied a floor loft in a building at 46 Chestnut Street. At this point, the firm of Cohn and Rosenberger had a difficult decision to make.

In order to increase sales, it needed to increase production. And with the increased production, it needed to increase profit. Despite the economy of 1929 and the shaky condition of Wall Street, the company decided to take a great risk by building a factory covering 100,000 square feet. This was a courageous move, supported by the firm's proven, twenty-five-year track record.

Coro plant at 167 Point Street, Providence.

The world began to recognize Cohn and Rosenberger finished jewelry products, marked simply "Coro." The name was a combination of the names of the two original founders, *Co* for *Cohn* and *ro* for *Rosenberger*. This was a name the company would use for many years, although it wasn't until 1943 that the name of the firm officially became Coro, Inc.

The 1929 gamble paid off; another 60,000 feet were added in 1945 — and 12,000 square feet were added in 1950. In just twenty years, the factory had grown to 172,000 square feet covering almost all of a square block. Coro had the largest, most modern jewelry factory in the world. This allowed it to employ over 3,500 persons at the peak of its power. To this day, the current residents of Rhode Island will tell you stories of their grandparents, mothers, fathers, aunts, siblings, and cousins who found employment at the factory located in Providence. Coro would provide a desperately needed source of income during the dark days of the Depression, and brought many other companies into the vicinity, helping to build a strong and vital Providence.

By 1940, there were over 1,000 jewelry companies in the area employing 25,000 people. Rhinestones were the jewels of choice and reigned supreme for the next twenty years.

ESPIONAGE

There was a complete diner around the corner from the Providence location where many of the jewelry factory workers in the vicinity would have breakfast or lunch, or coffee after work. There were just plain no secrets; everybody would know what anybody else was doing. It was a friendly atmosphere, reflective of a brotherhood that was the greatest part of the jewelry industry heart.

This fact must be taken into consideration when discussing the great "rubber mold caper" that began in the early 1930s up north in Canada. The rubber vulcanizing process had just been invented, and experiments were being conducted at a firm in Canada. Much to the Canadian firm's disappointment, its application for a patent on the first successful rubber mold was not granted, since it only related to the application technology of the already proven rubber.

In order to stay ahead of the competition, Coro was always alert and eager to try new methods to increase its efficiency and production. Royal Marcher, in his position as the vice president in charge of product development and marketing, kept his ear close to the ground. He eagerly interviewed the inventor and was much taken with the mold. His foresight, initiative, and follow-through made him eager to acquire the innovation. A gentleman's handshake was all that was needed to seal the purchase agreement.

With all the care given to an FBI case, a top-secret, concealed room was prepared in the front of the Providence plant and employees were carefully scrutinized and screened before they were enrolled in the covert operations. At the beginning, processing involved three steps to make a mold. An engineer was put in charge of the mold training program. Employees went swiftly to work to learn the process, and during that time they were able to improve the materials involved. Even the mold-making process was simplified.

The mold soon proved its pliability, allowing undercuts in the product that had not been possible previously. Now imaginary animals, figurals, and flowing, curving Art Nouveau lines could be executed. Designs began to come alive. Art Deco with its angular lines took a backseat as designers began to flow with the tides of fashion.

The miraculous mold allowed the curve to become the shape of reality. Since there was no patent, secrecy was of the uppermost importance. Loyal employees protected what was going on behind the closed doors for almost seven years. How hard it must have been in such a close-knit industry not to drop any hint of the new development.

Another Providence company, Trifari, started using the rubber mold in 1938. It was rumored that a former Coro employee had revealed the new process. No longer a secret, many companies jumped on the bandwagon to take advantage of the miracle of rubber. Today, rubber molds are used all over the world.

RHINESTONE CAMPUS

Larger than most universities, Coro opened its golden doors wide to accommodate the flow of students eager to study the jewelry trade in the world's biggest factory. Coro was dubbed the "Jewelry Campus." Here the students would be paid fifty cents per hour as unskilled workers and would participate in all aspects of jewelry production. For that magnificent sum, the workers could attend the practical jewelry college and learn a professional trade. Coro was an unusual college where no monetary tuition was paid, but instead offered hourly work that provided a paycheck and the opportunity to acquire a skill. The education was unbelievable. An affordable college in the Depression years, the hard times of the 1930s, when jobs and money were so scarce, was a wonderful promise of a better tomorrow. Coro offered low-paying salaries, but a thorough education. With the work experience gathered at the Coro plant, young men and women could go on to bigger and better jobs.

The golden doors would open, and graduating students, eager to utilize their new knowledge, flowed out to enter the jewelry trade. Many graduated to become designers or model makers, or formed their own jewelry companies. An expanding network of trained, skilled people spread through the jewelry industry like the roots of a mighty oak tree. There were, and are still, extensive alumni in the surrounding area. People are proud to talk about their learning experiences on the Rhinestone Campus.

The pay scale at Trifari was much higher, but a person had to go in with more experience. At Coro, a person was welcome to come in and learn while he or she earned. The doors were wide open; how far one went in school depended on the individual. How long one stayed at the "college," how much one learned, and what courses one would take were up to the individual. Coro was certainly a hands-on, practical trade school, and deserved to be called a jewelry college.

Coro lines included a broad range of designs done in volume and produced in all price levels, from 50-cent pieces for the five-and-dime stores to $100 pieces for the specialty shops. In 1946, sales were reported at $32,000,000 (in today's dollars that would equal the grand sum of $320,000,000).

There were four divisions of Coro in 1951. Each division had a production manager, sales force, general manager, and showroom. In essence, it was as if there were four companies working under the the same Coro umbrella. Coro Jewelry accounted for the greatest volume of sales, with pieces retailing in the range of $1.00 to $10.00. Corocraft pieces were being sold in stores for $10.00 to $50.00. Coro Pearls had simulated strands in stores priced from about $1.00 to $75.00. Coro Teens was aimed at the young crowd, and pieces were priced for its young pocketbooks at $1.00 to $10.00.

In 1957, the Rivocor building was erected to house the manufacture of Corolite jewelry, made with a new process. Superpure aluminum made each piece light but strong. Corolite was owned by Coro, Inc; Rivo S.A. of Locarno, Switzerland; and the former Armbrust Chain Company of Providence.

It was reported that for many years, 50% of costume jewelry bought was made by Coro. The jewelry boxes of the world were being filled with Coro products. With a reputation of quality, high styling, a wide variety, and realistic pricing, Coro peaked in 1960 with sales hitting $33,191,895.

Even though Coro had three of the largest manufacturing plants in the world, it had trouble filling and supplying the demand. When help was needed, the close-knit Providence jewelry industry would lend a helping hand, taking over production stages to help meet deadlines. Such manufacturers as Hedison, in the United States, and even foreign factories were called upon to help Coro. Best Plastics Company furnished Coro with beads, as did companies in Japan.

Because of their hunch in 1901, Cohn and Rosenberger created an empire that could now fill the jewelry display cases in all the department stores nationwide. Dazzling and sparkling displays of Coro jewelry could now be found, not only in the United States, but all over the world.

"Premiere...Jewels by Coro," 1947.

WORLD WAR II

During World War II, a sense of duty called upon the jewelry industry to use its manufacturing plants to make military supplies. In the spirit of patriotism, Coro approached Uncle Sam with an offer to volunteer the use of the plant and employees. At first the military smiled and waved off Coro, for after all who could imagine any jewelry firm as being able to assist in the war effort? Coro was persistent, and was allowed to help Uncle Sam by making ring sites for the Army and Navy. The manufacturing plant, mostly manned by women, was dedicated to the production of booster cups, gasket washers, primers, tracer ignitors, and fuse covers for the duration of the war.

Fuses for the Barton ordinance department were made in a factory in Keene. Many of the ordinance contracts and all quartermaster contracts were filled at the Providence facility. Rear Admiral D. C. Ramsey, Chief of the Bureau of Aeronautics, U.S. Navy, was so pleased with the ring sites that he told Coro in 1943, "You may take pride in knowing that your product is directly helping to develop expert marksmen for the Navy air arm."

When World War II ended, Coro immediately swung back into full production. It was still considered the jewlery college, but the wages being paid to employees had increased. Now another title was given the giant company, "Number One."

Coro had 75 to 80 designers creating 10,000 active items, from shoe buckles to jeweled glasses, from pipes to watches. To retain its status as number one, Coro was sending representatives all over the world to scour it for unique findings. Soon Coro was importing materials from all over the world. Findings were shipped from Japan, Germany, France, Czechoslovakia, India, and Switzerland. Plastics, red straw flowers, and glass beads were just a few of the items needed to entice the women of the world to buy Coro jewelry.

Salesman Mathew Verse saw a mustard seed brooch at a Kansas City jewelry store in 1954 and mailed it back to the home office. Coro created a version that became a big seller. Fifteen million copies of this brooch, which had a mustard seed enclosed in a crystal ball, were sold.

In early 1960, Coro was the wholesaler of Lewis Segal earrings. By 1965, 50% to 60% of Coro's products were earrings. There were ten people devoted to designing earrings that retailed at $1.00 a pair.

Stores would display these earrings on wooden racks that were placed on top of the display cases. Customers were always knocking the earrings off, and this caused a stock problem. This earring problem was the main subject of the day for the Coro employees. Even when eating lunch one day, plant production assistant Jack Feibelman's mind was working on the problem. He watched the restaurant waitress hook his order to one of the clips that were attached to a circular metal rim, and the circular earring rack was invented. Problem solved, no more counter mess or lost earrings.

RICHTON INTERNATIONAL

In July of 1969, the Richton International Corporation acquired 36% of the stock of Coro, Inc. By February of the next year, Coro's board of directors agreed to merge with Richton to become the Richton Jewelry Company.

The death of Coro began in 1979, when Richton sold its inventory, trademarks (including "Coro"), and other assets to K&M Jewelry, Inc. In November of that year, various sections of the Providence plant were closed down, and the mighty machines went silent. The heartbeat that once could be heard by thousands of employees was slowly dying.

It was just three weeks before Christmas in 1979 when the remaining 525 Coro employees received their termination notices. On December 27, 1979, all finished goods, inventory, displays, and trademarks were sold to Marvella, Inc. (a subsidiary of K&M).

On March 18, 1980, Chapter 11 bankruptcy was filed. For eighty years, Cohn and Rosenberger's dream had lasted, but the golden doors would no longer open onto the rhinestone campus.

CORO LIFE LINE: A CHRONOLOGICAL HISTORY

1900	Stern, Cohn and Co. in operation
1902	E. Cohn & Co. in business
1903	Cohn and Rosenberger firm is founded
1910	Company incorporates
1911	Cohn departs or dies
1911	Manufacturing at Coro begins
1913	Coro moves to Providence
1912	Stock is traded
1929	Stock goes public
1929	Providence factory is built
1930	Coro Duette is patented
1933	Corocraft operates in England
1934	Coro operates in Canada
1935	Chicago salesroom is opened
1938	Francois line is added
1943	Coro is incorporated
1943	Son Gerald Rosenberger becomes Coro president
1943	Taxco, Mexican silver jewelry factory is purchased
1944	Stock goes public
1967	Gerald Rosenberger dies
1969	Richton International Corp. acquires 36% stock
1970	Richton becomes Coro's parent firm
1979	K&M Jewelry buys inventory and trademarks
1979	Sections of Providence factory are shut down
1980	Richton sells to Marvella
1980	Richton files Chapter 11

Thumbnail Biographies

EMANUEL COHN

Emanuel Cohn was born in 1859 and became a New York City businessman by 1901. The next year, he started the firm of E. Cohn & Company on 508 Broadway, in the heart of downtown New York. He was the founder of Coro and worked hard those first ten years establishing a wholesale firm that supplied other jewelry manufacturers items directly to retail purchasers.

The greatest mystery is not how he founded the company, but how he left the company. He vanished in 1911 with no known published record of his demise. Some say he retired, some say he died; some believe he died the next year drowning during the sinking of the Titanic. His departure is an unsolved mystery.

All that is know for sure is that he left the Cohn and Roseberger firm that year. He left a wife and apparently no children. The family sold his interest to Carl Rosenberger, who was instrumental in taking the company to new heights.

CARL ROSENBERGER

Carl Rosenberger was born in Ruelsheim, Germany. His schoolteacher father instructed him during his elementary schooling, but he was restless and wanted to experience more. The brave young teenager decided to make his fortune in America.

The fourteen year old, fresh off the boat, went immediately to work for the jewelry firm of I. Weill and Company. By the time he was sixteen, he was a traveling salesman covering a territory ranging from Philadelphia to Chicago.

Two successful years were abruptly ended when the head of the firm died and the business was liquidated. Undaunted, Carl found immediate work with Newitter and Rosenheim, a jobbing jeweler. He continued gaining more jewelry experience for the next three years. He then went on to Fischel and Nessler. His early schooling at the hands of his father had formed his desire for knowledge, and he was stockpiling years of practicum in his chosen field, the costume jewelry industry.

During that time, in 1900, Emanuel Cohn and a partner started the Stern, Cohn and Company. The partners separated in 1902. Mr. Cohn began his own firm, E. Cohn & Company, and Carl Rosenberger joined the organization. Carl was now a married man with responsibilities and an ambition to make his mark.

Carl Rosenberger,
original partner and first president of Coro.

By 1904, Rosenberger had established his position and become a partner in the company that was now called Cohn and Rosenberger. For six years, the two men continued their profitable partnership. But in 1911 Cohn disappeared, and the family sold his business shares to Rosenberger. In less than ten years, young Rosenberg had found the path to the golden riches he had dreamed of when a young boy in Germany.

By hard work and ambition, he was now the head of a thriving business. He could, and would, establish a dynasty; his was a gold-plated success story. His door would always be open to all who were willing to work, a boost to the Providence locale. Today, fond stories are told by Rhode Islanders who remember the stories of their family members who earned their livelihoods working at the plant.

But Mr. Rosenberg's generosity did not stop there; he was a well-known philanthropist who contributed through memberships in civic organizations. An active member of the community, he was a Masonic member, serving as a director of the Temple Emanuel. He was an active sportsman. At the Metropolis Country Club, he played a fine game of golf. An avid horseman, he belonged to the Fulton Riding Club. His life was filled with great love for his family, his business, and his adopted country.

GERALD ROSENBERGER

Carl Rosenberger's son, Gerald, was born in New York in 1903. He attended primary and high school there. He received a college degree from the Wharton School of Commerce and Finance at the University of Pennsylvania and then went on to Columbia University to complete his formal education.

Son Gerald E. Rosenberger,
who succeeded as president.

At the age of nineteen, in 1922, he went to work at the New York Coro salesrooms. He spent the first eight years covering the far western territory before earning the important and prestigious appointment of salesman for the New York stores.

When salesman Jerome Oppehneimer became ill, Gerald took over the midwestern territory as well. He was chosen to accompany Henry Rosenblatt to Europe many times, and enjoyed touring the continent as part of becoming acquainted with Coro's overseas operations.

He was 21 years old when he met his future bride. The wedding ceremony took place in 1925. Their union was blessed with two daughters, Joan and Gerri.

Gerald and his family summered at a Mexican retreat and took the time to explore the lovely Mexico scenery. Of course Gerald managed to find some time to investigate and explore the large south-of-the-border jewelry industry.

He became the president of the Coro board of directors in 1944. For over forty years, he was an integral part of the company. On January 31, 1967, Gerald E. Rosenberger, chairman of the board of Coro directors, passed away.

Having devoted all of his professional life to Coro, it almost seemed destined that he should die on the job. He had just had a business lunch at the Empire State Building in the private luncheon room. Mr. Rosenberger pushed the elevator button, then fell to the floor. He had suffered a fatal heart attack. His sudden death left a void at Coro that could not be filled.

The third generation chose not to remain in the business. His widow and daughters sold Coro to Richton International. The times and the American jewelry industry were changing.

ROYAL MARCHER

Royal Marcher was born in New York City on September 25, 1889. His mother must have had an intuitive idea of the potential her son was born with and the important role he would play in the history of the jewelry industry when she gave him that special name.

He was schooled in New York public schools and continued his education at the high school of commerce. His early jewelry experience was earned at his first job, with Guthman Solomon.

In 1911 he joined Coro and became a salesman, quickly making a name for himself as charismatic, personable, and one cracker-jack salesman. In the 1920s, salesmen had several sample trunks. Their assistants were responsible for packing and shipping the valuable merchandise. Showrooms were set up along territorial routes and buyers from the local stores and shops would attend the "trunk shows." The latest hot fashion jewelry trends from New York were all brought to their hometowns.

Marcher was eventually put in charge of the firm's selling and most of its buying. He was elected to the Coro board of directors in 1918. In 1923 Royal Marcher maried, and soon a son, Royal, and a daughter, Jane, rounded out the family. The 1930s saw Marcher in charge of the offices and salesrooms in both Canada and Chicago.

He left his mark on Providence when he initiated the civic clean-up campaign. Today, the beautiful waterways of that city are refreshing reminders of the man. The Rhode Island School of Design has recognized Marcher's contributions to Providence and the state with the Royal Marcher Scholarship.

Vice president Royal Marcher.

ADOLPH KATZ

Adolph Katz could be said to be the epitome of the immigrant who found a golden path in America. It all started in Germany, in a small village, Fulda, where St. Boniface is buried. On March 4, 1906, it added one more citizen — Adolph.

He received all of his schooling in Germany and was able to attend the University of Frankfort, but his mother was raising two boys alone; he had to quit to start earning some money. At the age of sixteen, he found work on the Frankfort stock exchange floor. For two years, Adolph dreamed of going to America. He had an Uncle Katz in New York and had heard of the wonders of the big American city.

His future was uncertain in Germany, as the Nazi party was growing stronger and creating turmoil in his native country. He felt it was time to leave. Bravely, he journeyed to the land of opportunity and arrived at Ellis Island, with very little money in his pocket, speaking only broken English.

His uncle and aunt, who ran a restaurant, saw to it that Adolph had one good meal a day. It was very difficult for him to find a job, although he searched diligently for over a year. The disappointment made the year seem a lifetime.

Aunt Katz was heartbroken to see him suffering so. She had a brother who was a vice president of American Cigar and a close friend of Carl Rosenberger. Feeling sorry for her nephew, she asked her brother to see if there would be a job at Coro for Adolph.

And that is how the story goes. Katz started at Coro in the shipping department in New York City. The news from Germany was not good; Katz's brother had died, leaving his mother all alone. Grieving for her son and suffering from diabetes, she decided to get a visa and come to see her Adolph.

Her health continued to deteriorate. With her death, Adolph became an orphan. Royal Marcher heard of the plight of the young man and took him under his wing. Katz was made responsible for packing Marcher's sample cases and bags for his trips to Providence. With that simple gesture of friendship, Marcher initiated the start of Katz's rise from shipping boy to executive vice president and a member of the board of directors in 1944.

Katz learned much from Marcher, who was the guiding force of the sales division. Through the many trips he made with Marcher, he made numerous contacts with the men who sold Coro jewelry and the stores that bought Coro jewelry. He quickly became the broker between the New York offices and the Providence plant, an information conduit bringing and sharing what was on the drawing boards at the plant, what was selling, and what women in the various parts of the United States were wearing.

Although Katz was never a designer, he had a vital part in the selection of the designs to be featured in the upcoming major lines. In his position as plant manager with four supervisors, he played a vital role in the production side of Coro. His name can be found on many of the registered design patents as a representative of Coro.

The lonely immigrant found his chosen path through the golden doors.

JEROME H. OPPENHEIMER

Jerome H. Oppenheimer was a Valentine's Day arrival in 1891, at the home of his parents, Edwin and Leonore Oppenheimer. Jerome was married in the early 1900s, and the couple was blessed with two children, Jerome and Leonore, named after her paternal grandmother. The children enjoyed their early childhood in Brooklyn, New York, and attended school close to their home.

During his early manhood, Jerome worked at the notions departments of several stores. This gave him hands-on experience in selling goods and handling customers. By hard work and diligence, he was fortunate enough to enter partnership with the firm of Cohn and Rosenberger on January 1, 1910.

He had found his profession. He was made the traveling representative for the midwestern United States and Canada. As a young man on the road, he found himself enjoying trunk sales, or sales from his well-equipped trunks filled with Coro jewelry samples.

Then on he went to the southern United States before moving into the New York personnel office of Coro. He became a vice president and was elected to the board of directors in 1913. He served the board in the capacity of secretary for many years. World War II found him handling the military post exchanges.

In the tradition of other Coro leaders, he was involved in community welfare work and devoted his life to helping others.

HENRY ROSENBLATT

Henry Rosenblatt was born in Romania in 1886. He was very fortunate to acquire his schooling in both Romania and the United States. Majoring in language, he honed his gifted tongue and could speak nine or ten different languages, a gift that was to serve him well in his future.

In 1908, Mr. Rosenblatt joined Cohn and Rosenberger and was placed in charge of the receiving department. (After all, he could read all the foreign labels.) He received a very important job in June of 1919. He made his first European buying trip, and his position as a buyer lasted for twenty years. He made at least two foreign trips a year and made many strong jewelry connections in Europe.

Because of his language skills and extensive time spent on the Continent, Rosenblatt was responsible for organizing Coro's offices in England and Europe. In 1935, he established the Paris sales office.

As a member of the board of directors, he served an important function as the foreign connection. He kept abreast of what was happening overseas and updated the executive Coro officers.

He married in 1918 and was blessed with three daughters, Gloria, Janet, and Marjorie.

GEORGE ROSENBERGER

Another member of board of directors was the nephew of Carl Rosenberger, George Rosenberger. Born on November 21, 1892, in New York, he received all of his schooling in Manhattan.

Starting his Coro career early, at the age of sixteen, he took a factory job. He diligently counted the chatons imported from Swarovski. He went on to assist in the import department.

Uncle Carl introduced him to the life of a Coro traveling salesman, taking him on sales trips to the Midwest. George found the job of his dreams and continued on the road for over thirty-three years.

When at home, he was busy with his wife and two sons.

JACK FEIBELMAN

Jack Feibelman was born in Berlin, Germany, in 1920, and that is where he spent his early school years. They were peaceful years until the Nazi party began its march through the countryside. To escape the ravages of World War II, he left for America at the age of 16. Immediately, he searched for a way to support himself in New York City. He went to work at Bloomingdale's for the magnificent sum of $2.50 a day.

Then he heard about the Rhinestone Campus and entered through the golden portals at the age of 17. By 1938, he was the assistant controller in the Coro main office. He was to work there for four years before joining the army in 1942, training in the Miami Beach Air Corps Ground Squadron.

The Army Air Force administration put him through courses at the Colorado State College. At the end of World War II, this man who had seen the Nazi Germany beginning of the war and the United States ending of the war returned to civilian life.

The golden portals were wide open to returning war veterans. Feibelman was welcomed and became an assistant to Adolph Katz. He went on to become head of new product production in Providence.

Having earned his jewelry "diploma" from Coro, he decided it was time to graduate and enter the business world. In 1967, he started A&H Manufacturing Company, a jewelry carding facility in Providence.

Currently, Mr. Feibelman is a manufacturer's representative for a prime manufacturer, selling jewelry to wholesalers worldwide. He has never left the jewelry profession he chose in 1937, and is proud to be called a member of the Coro alumni.

Marketing

TRAVELING SALESMEN

In the beginning there was just one New York salesroom, where Cohn and Rosenberger stood ready to greet their wholesale customers. As the business grew, territories were assigned to a group of salesmen under the direction of Royal Marcher.

The class system at Coro ranked salemen at the top of the employee ladder, and everyone at Coro treated them with respect. Salesmen usually came from the pool of stockroom boys who had earned their promotions to the top. Coro had 75 salesmen on the road before permanent showrooms were established.

Large steamer trunks were packed with samples, and the men would travel to their assigned areas. Trunk sales held on location brought orders into the home office. It wasn't just the orders they brought back that made salesmen important to Coro; salesmen kept Coro at the front of the jewelry industry. Returning salesmen brought feedback from all over the United States, reporting on what was selling and what was not. They were important collectors of styles and colors that were being worn. Through their retail store contacts, they could advise the East Coast what the West Coast and Midwest were buying.

As the company grew, the decision was made to establish showrooms around the globe, where direct customer service would be available the year around. Salesrooms were quickly and strategically placed. In New York, the salesroom was at 47 West 34th Street and took up almost the entire block between 34th and 35th.

Cohn & Rosenberger showroom at 508 Broadway, New York, in 1901. Note the sign on the storefront.

Carl Rosenberger (behind the counter) is waiting on Fred Lazarus Sr., co-founder of F&R Lazarus of Cincinnati, Ohio.

SHOWROOMS AROUND THE WORLD

Showrooms were completely remodeled in 1939 and were considered by the entire industry to be the finest jewelry salesrooms in the world. Individual showrooms with air conditioning provided for the comfort of the buyers. The furniture was selected with painstaking care and with absolute disregard to expense. This is a 1939 photo of the Montreal salesroom located at 1255 Phillips Square.

Salesroom in Montreal, Canada, at 1255 Philips Square.

Chicago opened its salesroom in the heart of the Loop at 36 South State Street. This allowed manager Joe Kaim to be in a position to take care of all the Midwestern customers.

Los Angeles sales were centered at 607 South Hill Street; manager Sig Gams took the West Coast territory from Los Angeles to Denver. Dallas opened a salesroom in February 1945 at 116 South Poydras Street. San Francisco was the site of the Northwest office. Additional salesrooms were established in Atlanta and Miami.

Managers White and Barber supervised the London showroom at 1 Argyll Street beginning in 1933. The Paris office at 22 Rue St. George was manned by Keife and Company. There were offices in Germany and representatives in most of the Latin American countries. Now international customers could be served quickly. Stores in practically every major city in the world proudly displayed and sold Coro jewelry.

When Coro first opened its doors in 1901, there were few jewelry departments. By 1951, every store allocated important space to fashion jewelry.

Coro salesroom in New York City, at 47 West 34th Street.

Advice in the house booklet *A. B. C.'s of Selling Fashion Jewelry* was just one of the many special efforts Coro took to help the retailer promote sales. Eight steps to guide the jewelry departments in buying and selling techniques were listed. All the types of jewelry were explained, as were stone cuttings and settings. Royal Marcher was even known to travel to a store and work personally with staff to help arrange the jewelry departments.

Coro salesroom New York City, at 47 West 34th Street.

There were two major marketing events, the spring and the fall line showings. The complete creation of a line from beginning to end produced a major line. This required almost 3,000 new item samples, offered in all the colors and platings that could be ordered. Approximately 10,000 pieces would be on display, representing all the combined Coro divisions.

The creation of minor line, done twice a year, was the adding on of that which was acceptably popular and the dropping off of that which was not. In essence, Coro was cleaning the line.

There was always a market week for which company was working. The first Monday in January began the summer season, and the Fourth of July began the winter season. A market week was announced well in advance since the company had less than a year to prepare for the open house event and invite all the important retailers.

Coro slogans made strong statements supported by Coro's reputation and its long business history. "America's best dressed women wear Coro jewelry" said the company, and it produced advertisements to prove it. Stars Barbara Britton, Nanette Fabray, and Rosalind Russell were featured in Coro advertisements, as were many socialites such as Antonia Drexell Farle.

"Coro is the largest manufacturer of fashion jewelry in the world" was another slogan, and their factories in Rhode Island, Canada, and England were footage record holders. The three were monumental proof of the statement.

"Coro is the most widely know name in fashion jewelry" was a claim endorsed by shoppers.

"Coro pearls are the finest, most beautiful simulated pearls of all" ran an advertisment, and each pearl strand had lifelong luster.

Advertisements were placed in Vogue, *Harper's Bazaar*, *Life*, *Mademoiselle*, *Glamour*, *Seventeen*, *Photoplay*, *Charm*, and *Today's Woman*. "Worn the Most From Coast to Coast" was an advertising slogan back in 1940.

An additional slogan was "Coro is the largest manufacturer of fashion jewelry in the world." Coro, recognizing the importance of informing the public of its full lines of costume jewelry, devoted a great portion of its budget to advertising from the early 1940s to the late 1970s.

"America's best dressed women wear Coro jewelry...," 1947.

CORO TRADE NAMES

Throughout the years, Coro registered many names. The list that follows seems almost endless. The dates are taken from the first documented appearances of the names. The names are from three different labeling categories. The first category encompasses all the Coro divisions over its 80-year history (marked "D"). The second, specific groups of jewelry designs (marked "J"). The third category deals with merchandise employing patented, unique mechanical development (marked "M").

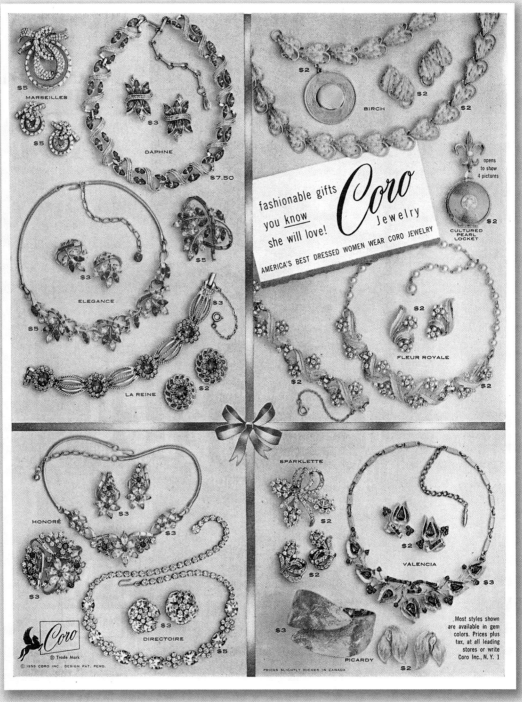

"Fashionable gifts…," 1955.

47 WEST . . . . D	DAILY DOUBLE (1951) . . . . .J
AJUSTA (1948) . . . . .M	DAY AND NIGHT (1940) . . . . .J & M
ALMANAC OF LIFE (1954) . . . . .J	DEBUTANTE (1933) . . . . .J
AMERICANA (1936) . . . . .J	DIAMOND-ITE (1960) . . . . .M
ANCESTRAL (1930) . . . . .J	
ANDRÉ (1937) . . . . .D	
ANGEL OF LOVE (1952) . . . . .J	
ARISTA . . . . .J	
ARISTOCRAFT (1950) . . . . .J	
AROSTA (1954) . . . . .J	
AS YOU LIKE IT . . . . .J	
ATOMIC (1945) . . . . .J	
BLACK BEAUTY (1946) (cameo) . . . . .J	
BLITHE BLOSSOM (1956) . . . . .J	
BLUE DANUBE (1929) . . . . .J	
CALYPSO . . . . .J	
CARRACA (1940) . . . . .J	
CELLINI (1942) . . . . .J	
CHARMERS (1959) . . . . .J	
CHATTER PINES . . . . .J	
CHERUBIN (1956) . . . . .J	
CHURCHILL DOWNS (1946) . . . . .J	
CLEOPATRA . . . . .J	
CLIP-EASE (1941) . . . . .M	
CLOUD DRIFT . . . . .J	
COCKTAIL SET (1947) . . . . .J	
COLLEGIATE (1940) . . . . .J	
COLOR A LA CARTE (1959) . . . . .J	
COLORAMA (1954) . . . . .J	
CONSTELLATION (1946) . . . . .J	
CONTESSA (1946) . . . . .J	
COQUETTE (1948) . . . . .J	
CORO (1933) . . . . .J & D	
CORO CHROME (1957) (finish) . . . . .M	
COROCRAFT (1933) . . . . .J & D	
CORO ELEGANTE (1944) . . . . .D	
CORO FASHION WATCHES (1988) . . . . . . .D	
CORO GRAMS (1926) . . . . .D	
CORO KLAD (1965) (plating) . . . . .M	DREAMBOAT 1958) .J
CORO LITE (1923) (aluminum) . . . . .M	DUETTE (1929) .J & M
CORO MAGIC (1947) . . . . .M	EAR CHARMERS (1956) . . . . .J
CORO ORIGINALS (1947) . . . . .J	ELECTRA TREMBLE (1931) . . . . .J
CORO RADIANCE (1932) . . . . .J	ELITE (1948) . . . . .J
CORO SUPREME (1943) . . . . .J	EMPRESS EUGENIA (1930) . . . . .J
CORO TEENS (1940) . . . . .J & D	FASHION FLAIR (1957) . . . . .J
CORO TOTS (1941) . . . . .J & D	FASHION SQUARE (1931) . . . . .J
COURT JESTER (1955) . . . . .J	FASHIONATA (1960) .J

Diamond-ite 1961.

FIREBIRD (1963) . . . . .J	ROUND THE CLOCK (1956) . . . . .J
FLYING TIGERS . . . . .J	SMART SET (1935) . . . . .M
FOR THAT PRICELESS LOOK (1944) . . . . . . .J	SODA SET (1957) .J
FRANCOIS (1937) . . . . .J & D	SOFT TOUCH (1959) . . . . .J
JEWELS BY FRANCOIS . . . . .J	SOUTHERN BELL (1946) . . . . .J
FUTURA (1953) . . . . .J	SPLENDOR (1948) .J
FUTURAMA (1953) .J	STAR-LITE . . . . .J
GIFT PAK (1953) . . . . .J	STERLING CRAFT . . . . .D
GLAMOUR (1940) . . . . .J	STOCKING STUFFER (1957) . . . . .J
GLAMOUR CRAFT (1958) . . . . .J & D	STYLED TO BEAUTIFY (1938) . . . . .J
GLITTER BOBS (1956) . . . . .J	SUBLIME (1948) . . . . .J
GRANDEUR (1950) .J	SUPREME (1948) . . . . .J
HI JINKS (1940) . . . . .J	TEENOGRAMS (1958) . . . . .J
IMPERIAL BOUQUET (1931) . . . . .J	TEMPT ME (1963) .J
JEWEL CRAFT (1920) . . . . .D	THE AVENUE (1925) . . . . .J
JEWELFULLY YOURS (1947) . . . . .J	THOROBREDS (1942) . . . . .J
JINGLE JANGLE (1958) . . . . .J	TICKLED PINK (1958) . . . . .J
JINGLE RINGS (1958) . . . . .J	TRAVELOGUE (1957) . . . . .J
LA BELLE (1963) .J	TRIO TRICKS (1951) . . . . .J
LOVABLE (1957) . . . . .J	TRIQUETTE (1937) . . . . .J
LOVE LOCKET (1953) . . . . .J	TWIN TONES (1954) . . . . .J
LUCKY BUCK (1949) . . . . .J	VALIANT (1948) . . . . .J
LUSTRALITE (1950) . . . . .J	VANITY FAIR (1948) . . . . .J
MAGIC EYE (1938) . . . . .J	VENDOME (1944 – 1979) . . . . .J & D
MAHARANI (1935) .J	VERITE (pearls) . . . . .J
MAHJONG (1923) . . . . .J	WHIRLAWAY (1949) . . . . .J
MAMIE (1952) . . . . .J	WOOD NYMPH (1963) . . . . .J
MEMORIES OF LIFE (1954) . . . . .J	
METALITE (1929) .M	
MOON BEAM (1956) . . . . .J	
MOON RAYS (1956) . . . . .J	
MUSIC BOX (1923) . . . . .J	
NIGHT OWLS (1944) . . . . .J	
NORSELAND . . . . .J	
OSCAR DE LA RENTA . . . . .J & D	
OUR LITTLE DARLING (1946) . . . . .J	
PADDOCK . . . . .J	
PARAGON (1946) . . . . .J	
PINAFORE . . . . .J	
PRESTIGE (1948) .J	
QUEEN BESS (1943) . . . . .J	
QUIK TRIK . . . . .J	
QUINTETTE (1938) . . . . .J	
QUIVERING CAMELLIA (1939) . . . . .J	
RAMBLING ROSES (1944) . . . . .J	
RAVEN (1963) . . . . .J	
REGALA (1948) . . . . .J	
ROMANTIC (1931) .J	

Verite Jewels, 1961.

Coro White 'n Hue.

Foreign Connections

ACROSS THE OCEAN

Coro made a major decision in 1933. The success of the Providence Plant and the sales of the Duette were leading the company into a need for growth. The company decided to manufacture and sell jewelry in Europe.

England was decided on as the base of operations for the European adventure. Now there was just one obstacle to hurdle. England would not permit the use of the name *Coro*. Its courts decided the name would be in direct conflict with the already established English firm Ciro. Ciro was a big name in England at that time and was well known on the Continent.

So the Sussex plant, which was almost as big as the Providence plant, produced Coro jewelry under the name of *Corocraft*. Strangely, Ciro was being sold in the United States and Ciro was indeed a customer of Coro at that time.

All designing was headed by Gene Verri and done stateside in the Providence plant. Duplicate rubber molds and product types were kept in Rhode Island. Some of the designs proved to be so popular that they were made in Providence and sold here in the United States.

It took almost 15 years before Sussex acquired its own design staff and did its own model making. All jewelry turned out by the plant was intended for sale within Great Britain.

Swarovski bought the Corocraft operations in London and Sussex, with the intention of using the Coro name to enter the European jewelry industry, around 1969. The undertaking proved to be somewhat of a fiasco, and Swarovski closed it down.

GERMANY

Coro established a purchasing office in Pforzheim, Germany, in the late 1920s. The American firm concentrated on buying manipulated merchandise from both Germany and Czechoslovakia. The goods were named for the Coro styles that incorporated beads.

World War II saw the closing of the office during the war years, but the office was reopened after the war ended.

JAPAN

In 1923, contact was made with the Japanese jewelry industry. Coro representatives inititated purchasing operations. Beads, pearls, and findings were fed to the American jewelry giant Coro. Also, samples of finished Japanese jewelry were sent to Rhode Island for possible design ideas.

World War II interrupted the flow of materials, but Eisenhower's revitalization efforts on behalf of the Japanese economy renewed the connection with Japan, bringing such items as the plastic gift box beads seen on the cover of this book.

Corocraft Ltd. plant in Crawlery, Sussex, England.

NORTH OF THE BORDER

In 1934, despite the Great Depression, or maybe because of the hard times, Coro made the decision to establish a presence in Canada. Our neighbors to the north accepted Coro with open arms.

The setup was under the supervision of Milton Gottlieb. The operation proved so successful that Toronto soon saw a large Coro facility on Botany Street duplicating the Providence manufacturing layout.

Since there was no design staff in Toronto, a delegation would come to Providence weekly to find out what was popular in the United States and take those products back to Canada. All jewelry manufactured in Canada would be sold in that country; there would be no exportation.

Bill Landy was the president of Coro Canada. He was a disciple of Royal Marcher and modeled his offices after Royal Marcher's smoothly run operations in New York and Rhode Island. Larry Metcalf was vital in the Canadian operations.

In April of 1939, a sales office was located at Wellington and York Street, Toronto, Canada. Coro continued the operation of the Canadian facility until 1970, when the Richton International Corporation filed Chapter 11 bankruptcy.

The Toronto connection successfully campaigned for the rights to the Coro, Vendôme, and Oscar de la Renta lines. Obtaining the archives of the three Coro divisions, it was able to produce the three lines from 1979 to 1984. For five years, it was able to keep those names alive and in the stores.

Despite its heroic efforts, the three lines were eventually discontinued and our northern neighbor closed the Toronto plant doors.

POSTSCRIPT

After Coro Canada closed, Larry Metcalf came down to the United States to help establish the Swarovski American program in Providence. Completing the project, Metcalf returned to Canada; he had another dream to undertake.

He had always wanted to hunt and take a black bear in Alaska. A plane flew him into a remote hunting spot. A long hike from the camp was rewarded when he bagged a large bear. Now the pilot and Metcalf had to get the bear back to the plane and fly the trophy back to camp.

Metcalf was exhausted when he finally got to camp and went to lie down to rest; he was never to get up again.

SOUTH OF THE BORDER

Gerald Rosenberger discovered a wonderful vacation spot south of the border and acquired a sunny hacienda as a retreat from the cares of managing Coro. Always a man to explore his location, he uncovered a fascinating Mexican business.

Not surprisingly, it was a well-run, prosperous jewelry studio in Taxco that produced silver items. This was in the 1940s, when the World War II war effort had made it necessary for Uncle Sam to declare all tin and lead production be dedicated to making much needed military supplies. This limited the lead available to the jewelry industry, reducing many companies to melting down old window sash weights in order to have some white metal for casting.

Mr. Rosenberger discovered a hidden silver mine when he met Taxco silversmiths such as William Spratling and Hector Aquilar. He quickly bought interest in one of the larger Taxco jewelry factories. The silversmiths used their expertise and incorporated the Coro techniques, meeting the high standards of quality required by Mr. Rosenberger. They produced many pieces for Coro's line of Mexican silver and gold-plated silver. Some of the pieces were marked "Made in Mexico," and all were marked "Coro."

This helped to round out Coro's wartime production. Hands across the border, the partnership helped Coro maintain its jewelry lines while helping on the homefront with the manufacturing of much needed items for the military forces.

The Taxco factory continued producing Coro silver for a term of approximately three years, helping out its North American friends.

Designing

CORO HEAD DESIGNER GENE VERRI

Designer Gene Verri in his Coro office, 1930.

The Italian influence behind the golden doors for over thirty years was Eugene Verrecchia, or Gene Verri, as he was better known.

A designer you don't recognize? Have you seen the Coro Duette? The twin birds on a perch, fur clips fitted into a brooch frame? The large blue-eyed owls, the bows, the flowers, the Quivering Camellia? All the work of this designing genius.

When the Verri designs were submitted to the patent office, petitioning for copyright, the official signing them on behalf of Coro was Adolph Katz.

Let me go back and properly introduce you to Gene. His parents came here from Italy in 1904. Mr. Verrecchia was a jeweler working for the best factories, such as Osby and Barton. Even though the couple had been blessed with the birth of twin boys in 1911, Alfeo and Eugene, Mr. Verrecchia and his wife were unhappy in the United States.

The Verrecchias had come from well-to-do families in Europe, and they found America to be a very primitive country. It seemed, to them, that most everybody who worked here was a mill worker. The factories ran long ten-hour days, and there was not much time left to spend on the finer aspects of life.

They wanted to leave for Scotland. They took the twins and their third son back across the ocean to make a new home in the Scottish highlands. Tragedy struck; the boys lost their mother, and World War I found their father a prisoner of war.

The children, now five in all, were motherless. They bundled up their small possessions and headed to America and their stateside relatives. The year was 1922, and 12-year-old Eugene worked hard, but also somehow found time to develop a love of art. By the time he was 14, he had a scholarship to the Rhode Island School of Design. He went on to win further honors while there.

All of his spare time was spend in the libraries of Providence and New York City to study fine art. Plainfield South, of Providence, frequently offered him employment. Finally, it offered him a deal he couldn't refuse: the magnificent sum of $18.00 weekly and the opportunity to continue his schooling and do all the art work for the firm.

Most of the jewelry being made in Providence in the 1920s was basically tool work and enameling. There weren't many designers available. It was now 1933, and Coro was looking for a young designer who could change the Art Deco style of the period.

Plainfield encouraged Gene to take the challenge. Within three months of his employment, Gene was discovered by Royal Marcher. Adolph Katz rounded up all of Gene's drawings done for Coro and carried them to Marcher's office. Marcher wasted no time in naming Gene the head designer, giving him a small office with a custom-built desk at the Providence factory. More importantly, he gave Gene the freedom to design whatever he wanted. At the age of 22, Gene had found his niche. He was placed in charge of the model room and the designing.

In those days his work mostly dealt with necklaces, brooches, and bracelets. Earrings were not very popular. There were no pierced earrings being made, just screw backs. Only a few companies were making clips, Coro, Monet, and Trifari.

In the late 1940s, Gene was the designer for the J. C. Penney's program Back to School and the Sears campaigns. For some 12 years, he was the only designer. However, he had an open-door policy to see freelancers. They would bring him their designs and he would always buy the designs to encourage them. Seldom were the designs used.

For thirty years, Gene turned his talents to creating jewelry. He drew his inspiration from nature — graphic, animated sea life. During his time at Coro, he saw many changes, including the advent of the rubber mold, Duettes, Coro pearls, mood rings, and plastics. In 1948, with permission from Coro, he started his own company. At first it was called Craftsman, then it was called Sample Art (with an "SA" logo), and finally it was named Gem-Craft Corporation.

Gene Verri persuaded his twin, Alfeo, who had the natural ability to coordinate colors, patterns, and findings, to join him. Gene, the model maker, with his knowledge of the mechanics and all the stages of jewelry making, worked hand in hand with his brother.

Work was done for Capri, R. Mandle, Tancer, Kramer, and Cadora, to mention a few. Gene continued working for Coro until 1965.

In 1975, Gene's son, Ron Verri, was called in to see inventor John Reynold's biofeedback silver ring. Ron would go on to create a mood ring for Gem Craft. Then, in 1976, he developed revolutionary hypo-allergenic earrings.

Ron had been running a digital pocket watch company, but he closed his watch line to devote his full time to the family business. Uncle, father, and son were now working closely together.

Alfeo Verrecchia died of cancer in 1978. Father and son, sharing a grand passion for jewelry, have continued to work together ever since. Each year they have 70 to 80 pads of jewelry, a line of 300 to 400 pieces ready for market twice a year.

In the year 2000, Gene Verri was honored by the Vintage Fashion and Costume Jewelry Club for his diamond 75th year of creating beautiful costume jewelry for the women of the world.

A limited edition of nine brooches was taken from his archives and re-introduced by Gem-Craft. These were marked "G. Verrecchia" and offered to members only.

Designer Gene Verri in his Gem-Craft office, 2004.

Included with the jewelry was a simple statement:

> For over fifty years Gem-Craft has been a leading creator of magnificent
> costume jewelry. Our jewelry is a collection that reflects innovative
> treatments. Much of the inspiration is European. We travel regularly to
> London, Paris and Milan. Some pieces are abstractions, others are
> interpretations of period jewelry — Grecian, Byzantine, Etruscan, estate
> art deco, Chinese and more. In each piece we strive to maximize the visual
> impact with cabochons, faceted stones and accents of enamel.
>
> We hope this article of jewelry will be a source of beauty and pleasure for
> you and your family.
>
> Gene Verrecchia, Gem-Craft.

Those who were fortunate enough to purchase the jewelry take pride in his artistry.

Ninety-three-year-old Gene Verri can still be found at his Cranston, Rhode Island, workbench at Gem-Craft. After almost eighty active years in the jewelry industry, he is still producing beauty.

Son Ron is completing 56 years with the company. Two generations with a family slogan, "Life is change, be ready to change. If you don't embrace change, you'll get left behind."

GENE VERRECCHIA LIMITED EDITION

*Brooch, heart, gold toned with
colored rhinestones and pearls of
various sizes. $50.00.*

*Horse head brooch, signed
"Robert Mandle," done in gold tone,
trimmed with rhinestones. $40.00.*

Face brooch, pre-WWII Coro production, with 220 chatons, 21 baguettes, 10 pear-shaped stones, and 1 square stone. $80.00.

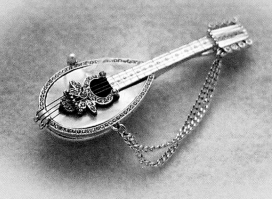

Mandolin Brooch, designed for Uri Mandle in 1938. Piano wires, faux mother-of-pearl, gold plated, diamente accents. $45.00.

Retro brooch, textured gold tone, with ruby cabochon. $40.00.

Retro brooch, emerald cabochon, aurora borealis and ruby rhinestones. $45.00.

Retro brooch, with three green pear-shaped crystals, aurora borealis rhinestones, rose gold tone. $45.00.

Retro brooch, silver tone, Montana blue cabochon. $40.00.

Brooch, designed for Capri, has 220 chatons and 5 black baguettes. $70.00.

The full set of nine brooches, priceless.

The Birth of Costume Jewelry

CORO JEWELRY

A designer would draft the piece of jewelry being proposed and submit the idea for approval. The design would be judged on the basis of current fashion trends, general appearance, ease or complexity of design, manufacturing cost, and retail pricing. Additional consideration had to be given to placement in one of the numerous Coro lines, along with the schedules of the spring and fall merchandising shows.

If the creation passed all criteria, it was then returned to the designer for a complete drawing that showed a full rendition of the projected piece as it would be seen from all directions...top, bottom, and both sides. Full attention was given to the rhinestones, stones, beads, colors, and findings needed to breathe life into the creation.

The design was then entrusted to the model maker, an artisan who would sculpture a full-scale model in careful detail. The model was thoroughly examined before being committed to the gentle hands of the department that fashioned the master rubber mold.

White metal pieces were usually made by the casting method that required wax molds be made of the master rubber mold, but brass pieces were stamped.

WHITE JEWELRY

White metal was melted down to a liquid form that was poured into the crevices of the mold. The metal hardened and conformed to the design. All rough edges were then trimmed away.

The next stage was polishing to eliminate the scratches and rough edges. Polishing increased the highlights of the design and brought out the natural luster of the base metal. Then it was time for the fastenings to be soldered on.

If the company logo had not been placed on the mold, this was another opportunity when the manufacturer could give the piece a name by stamping, or by soldering on a cartouche.

The naked, newly formed piece then headed for the plating room to receive its first clothing. It was given a bath of copper and a heavy coating of bright nickel. The top blanket was the final covering of the desired color (e.g., silver or gold).

Coro introduced flash plating in the late 1940s. White metal jewelry had a glue binder coat applied and then received a spray metal covering in much the same manner that cars are painted. This allowed a larger number of items, in fact a roomfull, to be sprayed at one time. If when examining a piece of Coro you notice that the plating is worn and you can see the base metal, suspect that this was a post–World War II production piece.

Any enameling would be done at the next station. The chosen color would be sprayed on and then baked on in a 250-degree oven to give the piece a coating that could survive for years.

The piece then went on to the stone setting room, which was filled with the glittering rhinestones, glass or plastic stones, and beads that would enhance the beauty of the new creation. All that was left now was the packaging.

BRASS JEWELRY

All brass pieces were made by the stamping process, with dies. A die set had two parts, the dire (front) and the forcer (back). Sheets of brass were inserted between the two parts of the die, and by use of a drop hammer, the next step began.

A brass blank was converted into a design that was later pierced and trimmed. It then went through a series of operations, such as soldering, to connect the joints and put on the catches for the pins. Polishing increased the highlights of the design. It also eliminated scratches and rough edges, giving a luster to the base metal. Next came the plating of a heavy coating of copper, and then a heavy coating of nickel. Nickel coating was a step Coro added to prevent tarnishing before the metal plating was added. Lacquer was applied, and then the piece was baked in a 250-degree oven to give the laqure more durability. Stone setting was the final production step.

The following pictures were taken in Coro's Providence plant in 1930.

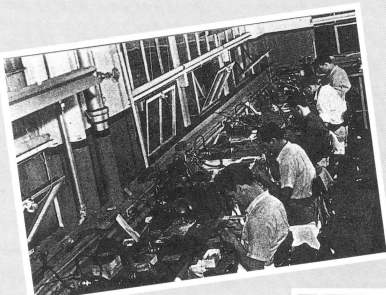

Sample and model makers.

Tool room.

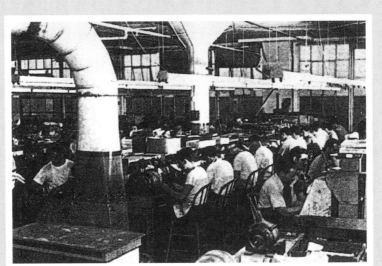

Polishing.

Plating.

*Lacquering
room.*

Stone setting.

Pearl room.

Logos as they would appear on the back of jewelry. Year of use is indicated whenever possible.

1921.

1919.

1945.

❧ *Jellie Bellies* ❧

Marlin with Lucite belly. $650.00.

Swan with Lucite belly. $350.00.

Turtle twins with Lucite belly. $425.00.

"Twinkling Twins by Coro," 1942.

*White lily of the valley
plastic necklace.*

Matching bracelet…

❧ *Three-piece parure, $135.00.* ❧

*with lily of the
valley earrings.*

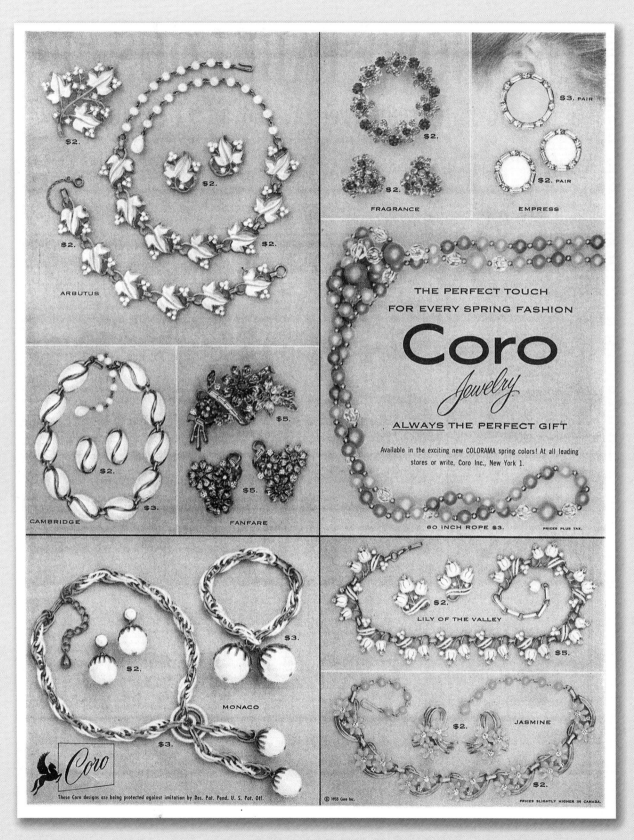

"The Perfect Touch…Coro," 1955

Gold-plated, gold and brown tone crystal bead necklace.

Matching bracelet…

and earrings.

❧ *Three-piece parure, $155.00.* ❧

*Red rhinestone
gold-plated
necklace.*

*Design repeated
in earrings...*

❧ *Three-piece parure, $180.00.* ❧

and in the brooch.

Necklace with blue chatons that alternate with blue rosette flowers.

Pattern carried over to bracelet...

and to earrings.

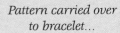

❧ *Three-piece parure, $235.00.* ❧

*Amber rhinestone,
mabé pearl necklace...*

with bracelet...

and earrings.

❧ *Three-piece parure, $145.00.* ❧

*Necklace with diamenté rhinestone
flowers and black enamel leaves.*

*Pattern repeated
in bracelet...*

and finished with earrings.

❧ *Three-piece parure, $195.00.* ❧

*Pink novelty bead and
leaf necklace...*

has a bracelet...

and earrings.

❧ *Three-piece parure, $165.00.* ❧

*Gold-plated, diamenté
baguette necklace...*

with the earrings...

and the brooch.

❧ Three-piece parure, $210.00. ❧

"Embraceable…" 1948.

*Yellow plastic flower
and chain necklace.*

Yellow plastic bracelet.

❧ *Three-piece parure, $125.00.* ❧

*Double yellow plastic
flower earrings.*

Antiqued gold-plated, mabé pearl, orange and blue rhinestone necklace.

Pattern repeated on brooch...

❧ *Three-piece parure, $175.00.* ❧

complimented by earrings.

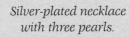

*Silver-plated necklace
with three pearls.*

*Matching
earrings.*

❧ *Set, $90.00.* ❧

*Silver-plated bracelet with
molded plastic buds.*

Matching earrings.

❧ *Set, $90.00.* ❧

*Amber, topaz, and green navette
rhinestone necklace…*

and earrings…

with a brooch.

❧ *Three-piece parure, $200.00.* ❧

*Silver-plated, pearl and
aurora borealis blue chaton
rhinestone necklace…*

has earrings…

and a bracelet.

❧ *Three-piece parure, $250.00.* ❧

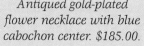

*Antiqued gold-plated
flower necklace with blue
cabochon center. $185.00.*

*Flowers repeated, one large
and four small on brooch.
$75.00.*

*Brooch with same flower,
one large and two small
blossoms. $55.00.*

*Same flower
repeated four times.
$65.00.*

*Necklace with gold-plated leaves, light
and dark green chaton rhinestones...*

with earrings...

and bracelet.

❧ *Three-piece parure, $195.00.* ❧

Brooch, gold-plated, lavender and amethyst navettes with purple baguettes.

Earrings even copy the drop.

The articulated necklace carries on the theme.

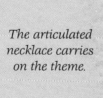

❧ Three-piece parure, $295.00. ❧

*Gold-plated necklace,
amber and gold
cabochons.*

Matching earrings.

❧ Set, $85.00. ❧

*Silver-plated, orange
rhinestone necklace…*

*and matching
earrings.*

❧ Set, $75.00. ❧

*Gold-plated amber and
brown rhinestone necklace.*

*Matching
earrings.*

❧ *Set, $85.00.* ❧

*Love birds
gold-plated
necklace.*

*Matching
earrings.*

❧ *Set, $85.00.* ❧

*Silver-plated necklace
with blue rhinestones…*

*has matching
earrings…*

*and Coro
presentation box.*

Boxed set, $145.00

Lariat necklace.

❧ Set, $75.00. ❧

Matching earrings.

Coro textured-print presentation box.

Blue aurora borealis necklace and earrings.

❧ Boxed set, $125.00 ❧

"Coro brilliant jewelry in three beautiful colors…"

*Necklace with gold-plated
chain and yellow plastic
daisies....*

*and accompanied
by earrings.*

❧ *Set, $45.00.* ❧

*Gold-plated necklace with
sapphire baguettes and
diamenté chaton rhinestones...*

*with
earrings.*

❧ *Set, $175.00.* ❧

Silver-plated, faux alexandrite necklace.

Drop earrings.

❧ *Set, $195.00.* ❧

Aurora borealis necklace...

and earrings.

❧ *Set, $95.00.* ❧

Double-strand, silver-plated braid necklace...

accompanied by earrings.

❧ *Set, $105.00.* ❧

Blue plastic flower necklace...

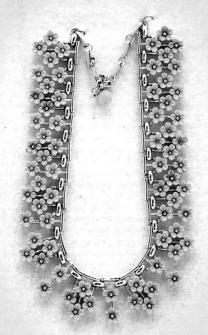

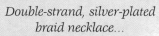

accompanied by earrings.

❧ *Set, $55.00.* ❧

"Created to flatter…Coro."

*Blue chaton rhinetsone,
mabé pearl, antiqued
silver necklace.*

Earrings.

❧ *Set, $75.00.* ❧

*Gold-plated, diamenté
rhinestone necklace.*

The earrings.

❧ *Set, $95.00.* ❧

Necklace of 11 fans, gold-plated, with red and clear rhinestones.

It has a bracelet.

❧ *Set, $95.00.* ❧

Blue and topaz necklace. $35.00.

Silver-plated, light and dark green chaton rhinestone necklace. $45.00.

*Gold-plated, topaz
rhinestone
necklace. $38.00.*

*Locket encrusted
with faux ruby and
turquoise. $55.00.*

*Gold-plated open rose with
diamenté rhinestone.*

❧ *Set, $68.00.* ❧

Matching earrings.

*Silver circular brooch, with
light blue rhinestones...*

*and matching
earrings.*

❧ Set, $45.00. ❦

*Enamel flower
brooch...*

*with
earrings.*

❧ Set, $45.00. ❦

*Bird with emerald green
belly and enamel head,
wings, and tail.*

Matching carded earrings.

❧ *Set, $75.00.* ❧

*Blue-bellied
lovebirds.*

Matching earrings.

❧ *Set, $95.00.* ❧

71

with earrings.

Pair of white enamel birds...

❧ Set, $95.00. ❧

*Wreath of white flowers
and green leaves...*

*has earrings
to match.*

❧ Set, $85.00. ❧

*Multicolored rhinestone brooch,
with antiqued gold finish...*

and earrings.

❧ Set, $68.00. ❧

*Brooch with silver
finish, blue enamel
spray, diamenté,
and rhinestones.*

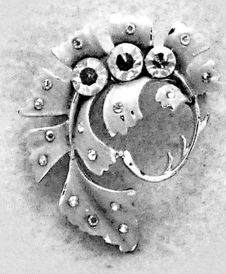

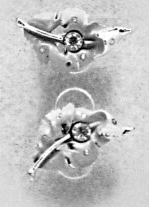

*Matching
earrings.*

❧ Set, $65.00. ❧

*Cuckoo Clock with
movable chain, decorated
with rhinestones.
$185.00.*

*Silver fountain
complete with
bird. $225.00.*

*Gold-plated female bust
with red and black
enamel stripes. $55.00.*

*Decorated heart
brooch. $95.00.*

Water carrier, green rhinestone buckets. $165.00.

Sword chatelaine can be worn as two pieces. $185.00.

Round brooch with topaz, black, and clear rhinestone. $45.00.

Snowflake brooch with black diamonds and clear rhinestones. $48.00.

Gold-plated bow, decorated with flowers. $28.00.

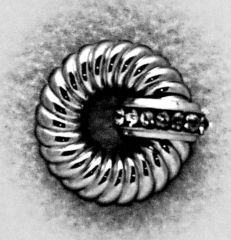

Gold-plated brooch with aquamarine rhinestones. $35.00.

Silver openwork flower brooch. $30.00.

Pair of small scatter pins.
$10.00 – 15.00 each.

Gold-plated heart brooch
with diamenté chaton
rhinestones. $68.00.

Two swords.
Pair, $45.00.

Fleur-de-lis brooch. $15.00.

*Clear and light and dark blue
rhinestone brooch. $22.00.*

*Brooch with topaz center
framed with pearls and
rhinestones. $18.00.*

*Silver-plated, diamenté rhinestone
nosegay brooch. $45.00.*

Sapphire blue and pink crystal gold-plated swan. $95.00.

Grey pearl–bellied swan. $145.00.

Pair of blue-bellied bird brooches. $65.00.

Mabé pearl–bellied seahorse. $45.00.

Silver flower brooch.
$28.00.

Clear cabochon flower brooch. $35.00.

Plastic Chinese face
brooch. $25.00.

Tiny ladybug. $15.00.

*Green enamel
fruit. $20.00.*

Aurora borealis duckling. $35.00.

*Gold-plated cat
head. $22.00.*

*Peacock brooch with
blue aurora borealis
rhinestones. $35.00.*

Male ballet dancer.
$30.00.

Gold-plated, enamel-
turbaned native. $45.00.

Japanned bee
studded with clear
rhinestones.
$45.00.

Gold-plated door knocker. $95.00.

Sea turtle, gold-plated, with red and black enamel trim. $195.00.

Blue enamel carnation brooch. $68.00.

Cat head with topaz ears, green eyes, and ruby-colored rhinestone nose. $28.00.

*Silver-plated, aurora borealis blue
rhinestone brooch. $25.00.*

Gold-plated starfish. $28.00.

Double dogwood brooch. $35.00.

Green rhinestone bud brooch. $25.00.

*Golden ribbon bow
brooch. $45.00.*

*Silver-plated, light and dark blue
rhinestone brooch. $35.00.*

*Satin and polished
gold-plated brooch.
$22.00.*

Crystal Question Mark brooch
with sapphire rhinestones. $48.00.

Silver-plated
aquamarine rhinestone
flower brooch. $35.00.

"Question Mark by Coro."

Gold-plated, ruby red
navette brooch. $55.00.

*Enamel peacock brooch
with multicolored
rhinestones. $48.00.*

Silver pelican. $125.00.

*Lavender enamel corn-
flower brooch. $75.00.*

*Brooch with enamel
orange daisies. $55.00.*

*Enamel flamingo.
$295.00.*

*Blue enamel flower
brooch. $55.00.*

*Gold-plated blue enamel flower
brooch with diamenté rhinestone
spray. $275.00.*

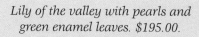

Lily of the valley with pearls and green enamel leaves. $195.00.

Yellow enamel tulip brooch. $150.00.

Silver brooch with diamenté rhinestones. $28.00.

Pearl caterpillar brooch. $35.00.

Brooch, red enamel fingernails on hand that wears diamenté rhinestone ring and bracelet with large emerald crystal. $275.00.

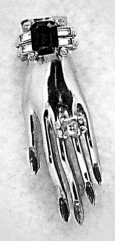

Diamenté pinwheel brooch. $85.00.

Brooch, lady leading gray hound. $125.00.

Modern lady leading small dog. $75.00.

Key and door knocker chatlaine. $225.00.

Door knocker brooch. $95.00.

Diamenté and rhinestone key with multicolored rhinestone accents. $185.00.

Key with faux turquoise beads. $85.00.

Brooch, gold-plated key with rose. $65.00.

*Gold-plated, lavender
and amethyst baguette
brooch. $85.00.*

Square silver-plated brooch. $65.00.

Golden brooch with two faux pearls. $45.00.

Golden feather. $25.00.

Gold-plated, green and blue baguette rhinestone brooch. $48.00.

Left: rhinestone lizard. $295.00. Right: white enamel cat with square red rhinestone–tipped whiskers. $250.00.
Courtesy of Ira Scheck.

The same cat with clear-tipped whiskers and a pewter finish. $175.00.

Royal Indian elephant. $350.00.
Courtesy of Ira Scheck.

Mexican strolling musician.
Courtesy of Ira Scheck.

South-of-the-border enamel senorita.
Courtesy of Ira Scheck.

❧ *Pair, $795.00.* ❧

Bacchus mask, black enamel accented with diamenté rhinestones. $695.00.

Diamenté rhinestone fuchsia blossom. $125.00.

"The perfect jewel of a gift...Coro..."

Mabé pearl, blue stone bracelet. $35.00.

Silver leaf bracelet with sapphire blue rhinestone clusters. $55.00.

Topaz and light blue rhinestone bracelet. $45.00.

Topaz and champagne rhinestone bracelet. $35.00.

*Art Deco bracelet.
$30.00.*

*Silver and light
blue rhinestone
bracelet. $40.00.*

*Blue and pink
rhinestone bracelet.
$30.00.*

*Pink and sapphire
rhinestone silver
bracelet. $35.00.*

Birthstone bracelet.
$65.00.

Pink rhinestone
silver bracelet with
hangtag. $85.00.

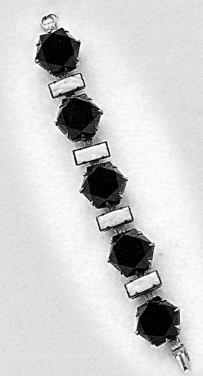

Large amethyst chaton
and pink bar spacer
bracelet. $125.00.

"She's got stars in her eyes...Coro."

Green novelty glass bracelet...

❧ Set, $65.00. ❧

*has matching
earrings.*

*Silver bracelet, with blue
rhinestones and dangling blue
crystal beads.*

❧ Set, $65.00. ❧

Matching earrings.

Silver leaf and light blue rhinestone bracelet...

❧ *Set, $85.00.* ❧

and matching earrings.

Antiqued gold-tone orange and green rhinestones bracelet...

with earrings.

❧ *Set, $78.00.* ❧

White plastic flower bracelet.

❧ Set $55.00. ❧

*Top: back magnet. Right: front plastic
flower earring. Bottom: the magnet back
of flower that touches the front of ear.*

Fur clip peacock. $65.00.

Gold-tone and enamel flower fur clip. $75.00.

Coro earring presenation box.

Gold and orange crystal shoulder duster earrings.

❧ Boxed, $155.00. ❧

*Black enamel, amber rhinestone
earrings. $10.00.*

Silver hoops. $12.00.

*Emerald green baguette
and chaton earrings.
$18.00.*

*Gold-tone and diamenté
rhinestone earrings. $20.00.*

*Diamenté rhinestone earrings
with gold-tone petals. $18.00.*

*Gold-plated sapphire blue
rhinestone earrings. $18.00.*

*Silver and pearl
earrings. $10.00.*

*Silver leaf and light blue
rhinestone earrings. $18.00.*

*Gold-tone, ruby and clear
rhinestone earrings. $15.00.*

*Light blue rhinestone
earrings. $10.00.*

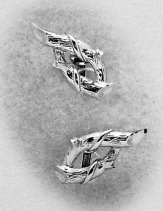

Gold bamboo earrings. $8.00.

*Watermelon fruit salad
earrings. $20.00.*

*Green rhinestone chaton
earrings. $15.00.*

*Faux turquoise beaded
blossom earrings. $20.00.*

Light pink earrings.
$15.00.

Emerald rhinestone
gold-tone earrings.
$15.00.

Golden cartwheel
earrings. $15.00.

Golden crown with
pearl earrings.
$28.00.

Red button earrings. $10.00.

Opaline and ruby rhinestone earrings. $18.00.

Earrings with large emerald green crystal circled with pearls. $18.00.

*Plastic white and
lavender earrings.
$8.00.*

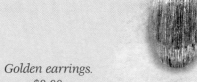

*Golden earrings.
$8.00.*

Carded earrings. $15.00.

Silver, blue aurora borealis rhinestone earrings. $15.00.

Gold-plated plastic flower earrings. $10.00.

Silver, blue rhinestone earrings. $10.00.

Silver, diamenté rhinestone earrings. $30.00.

Silver leaf with diamenté cluster earrings. $15.00.

Aurora borealis rhinestone earrings. $20.00.

Diamenté rhinestone earrings. $40.00.

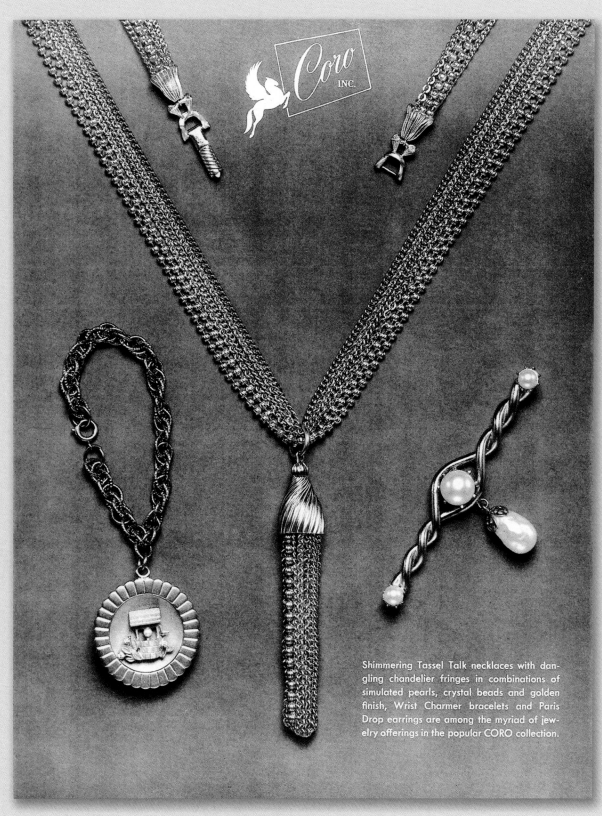

Shimmering Tassel Talk necklaces with dangling chandelier fringes in combinations of simulated pearls, crystal beads and golden finish, Wrist Charmer bracelets and Paris Drop earrings are among the myriad of jewelry offerings in the popular CORO collection.

Coro Shimmering Tassel Talk, 1961.

CORO STERLING

1942.

❧ *Logos as they would appear on the back of jewelry. Year of use is indicated whenever possible.* ❧

*Aladdin's Lamp
chatelaine with draped
chain and tassel, sterling
with gold wash. $185.00.*

*Sterling with gold wash basket
topped with bow and filled with
grape cabochons. $85.00.*

*Carousel with horses, accented
by multicolored rhinestones.
Sterling vermeil. $195.00.*

*Sterling vermeil penguin with
black enamel body and amber
glass belly. $295.00.*

*Masted ship, sterling with
gold wash. Silver sail with
diamenté and ruby
rhinestones. $190.00.*

Hoop-skirted woman with moon cabochon face. Red rhinestones in nosegay and skirt. $205.00.

Retro sterling silver vermeil with large ruby-colored cabochon. $180.00.

Man in the moon, red cabochon head. Diamenté accents. Sterling vermeil.

Matching clip-back earrings.

❧ Set, $350.00. ❧

*Sterling vermeil butterfly,
emerald green navettes and
diamenté rhinestones. $110.00.*

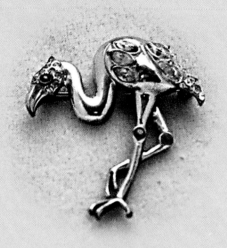

*Vermeil, stork
studded with colored
rhinestones.
$145.00.*

*Vermeil fur clips. Three
emerald navettes on each.
Pair, $110.00.*

Trio of vermeil flowers with multi-colored navettes. $95.00.

Vermeil bug with blue, green, and aurora borealis rhinestones. $85.00.

Royal crown with one ruby red and two emerald green cabochons. Multicolored rhinestones. $150.00.

Sterling heart, dove, and olive branches. $68.00.

Sterling birds. $125.00.

Sterling birds signed "Norseland by Coro." $155.00.

Sword chatelaine in sterling vermeil. Can be worn as two pieces or with sword in scabbard. $225.00.

Sterling fish. Enamel and pavé accents. $495.00.

Sterling vermeil, three blossoms with green chatons and diamenté rhinestones. $110.00.

Enameled marlin.
$395.00.

Sterling diamenté royal
crown. $165.00.

Lyre studded with
diamenté rhinestones and
two blue crystals. One of
the Philharmonic
Orchestra set. $170.00.

Diamenté gift basket, sterling. $130.00.

Sterling crown with three large chatons. $195.00.

Tailored sterling brooch. $85.00.

Chinese water carrier, green chaton buckets, vermeil. $205.00.

Vermeil prancing horse. Ruby navette ears, diamenté baguette mane. $150.00.

Four-flower vermeil sterling brooch.

Matching blossom earrings.

Set, $165.00.

Ferry boat, vermeil, stacks topped with multicolored pear-shaped stones. $175.00.

Trio of flowers, many colored navettes, vermeil. $105.00.

Retro cabochon brooch, vermeil. $135.00.

CORO TEENS

1940, front...

and back.

❀ *Logos as they would appear on the back of jewelry. Year of use is indicated whenever possible.* ❀

Brooch, candy apple on stick. $75.00.

Note "Coro Teens" hangtag.

CORO DUETTES

It all began in the Paris fine jewelry trade. At the time, there was hardly any market for costume jewelry in Europe. The fashionable ladies all wore precious metal and gemstone jewelry to adorn their dresses. Only fast ladies of the night and actresses wore flashy rhinestones.

It was in the Roaring Twenties that French jeweler C. Rothman introduced the first of the clever Duettes in diamonds. All of his creations were done in precious stones, never, never in imitation. His jewelry pieces were convertible and could be worn several different ways. A design featured individual designs that nestled together on a frame and could be worn as a brooch. If a lady so desired, the piece could be taken apart and the separate pieces could be worn as dress or fur clips. The clips could be used singly or in pairs. A pair strategically placed at each corner of a dress could create a square neckline. Just one unit that allowed the owner to wear it so many ways! French ingenuity created the Duette, and a wonderful sales promotion made it a success.

One day in 1929, Rothman's French representative packed his sales trunk with the season's collection and made for the United States. Fresh off the boat, he headed for the New York offices of Cohen and Rosenberger to make his presentation. After all, it was the biggest jewelry company in the United States and was very receptive to new ideas.

Vice president of sales and marketing Royal Marcher had an almost uncanny instinct for predicting what could sell, and was quick to seize the moment. The two men went immediately to a patent lawyer and then on to Washington, D.C. Just that suddenly, Coro became the only company to make Duettes. U.S. Patent Number 1798867 was given to the Duette mechanism, under the name of Gaston Candas, on May 31, 1930.

The first factory run had 18 to 20 styles, all rhodium plated. The Duette started out a challenge to designer Gene Verri to create a drawing and make a master model that could be manufacured. Bees took wing, birds nestled on a perch — the theme was always done in twos or threes. Sometimes they would fit side by side, sometimes sideways with the bottoms of the clips meeting; flowers would intertwine. The instructions had to be given for the frame to be customized to accomodate the fur or dress clips. Each frame had to be configured individually.

It started out as an idea that didn't have much support among the sales force. The men hadn't had much success out in the field with their Duette samples. Marcher went to a sales meeting in New York with a sample Duette in his pocket. Bringing the sample into full view, he made the statement that he had sold one of the big stores 36. Surely the salesmen could do the same. He sparked the sales force and ignited the Duette's popularity.

Holding full patent rights and license, Coro, with over 75 designs, reigned over Duette sales for 17 years, the length of time its patent rights protected the mechanism. Any company who dared to produce an imitation Duette was quickly taken to court by Royal Marcher. Coro's patent was air-tight, and the company won every case.

Design patents were also applied for. Quivering Camellia had the design patent number 110296. Remember, a regular patent is on the mechanism and a copyright is on the design. From 1954 on, the c in a cirlce copyright symbol was used on Quivering Camellias.

Duette designs had to be rendered in full color at the Coro plant. Each Duette creation had to be fitted with a custom-designed pin frame. Each frame was the product of one man working with a scroll saw to cut out the openings that would allow the two or three fur clips or dress clips to rest on the rim. This was a time-consuming process, but it accounted for the beautiful fit that allows the two clips to nestle so closely side by side. Advertisements proudly proclaimed, "A brooch so smart...now clips when apart."

From 1929, to 1946 Duettes were at the top of Coro's line. In 1940, the Duettes were selling retail for $5.00 to $9.00 each. Marcher's leading salesman, Abe Pollack, racked up so many sales that he bought a brand new motor car. And what did his license plate proudly proclaim? Yes, stock number "5757," for the horse Duette that had made it all possible. His wife, Anna, proudly wore her own Coro horse set as they toured New York in their brand new motor car.

Coro DUETTE

1929.

DUETTE

❦ Logos as they would appear on the back of jewelry. Year of use is indicated whenever possible. ❦

Early advertisement for Coro Duettes.

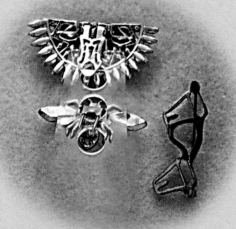

Top: back of dress clip.
Bottom left: back of fur clip.
Bottom right: Duette frame.

Round Duette, green navettes
with diamenté rhinestones.
$295.00.

The circle has been
separated. Top shows the
back of the dress clip,
bottom shows the frame
exposed when half has
been removed.

Each half of Duette has six amethyst chatons with pavé rhinestones. $275.00.

Twin enamel bees, gold plated, rhinestone wings. $350.00.

Twin diamenté baguettes and chaton rhinestones. $195.00.

*Two diamenté rhinestone birds
with enamel feathers and
flowers. $225.00.*

*Pair of large
blue chaton-eyed owls,
enameled feathers.*

*Matching
earrings.*

❧ Set, $350.00. ❧

*Enamel birds with
diamenté trim on a heart
background. $425.00.*

*Two clam shells with ribs of
red baguettes. $395.00.*
Courtesy of Ira Scheck.

*Enameled flowers.
$395.00.*

*Gold-plated, diamenté and red
baguette rhinestone Duette
with red enamling. $395.00.*

*Gold-plated flowers edged in
diamenté rhinestone; center is
sapphire navettes. Matching earrings.*
Courtesy of Ira Scheck.

❧ *Complete set, $595.00.*

Openwork petal blossoms with red rhinestone centers. $295.00.
Courtesy of Ira Scheck.

Pair of nosegays with sapphire navettes. $325.00.

Light blue chaton flowers. $395.00.

*Two sets of floral flowers. Red
in gold plate and sapphire in
silverplate. $295.00 each.*
Courtesy of Ira Scheck

*Red baguettes
explode out of
golden flowers.
$295.00.*

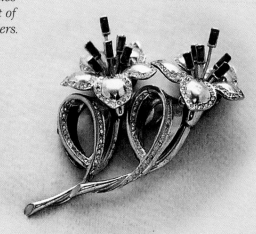

*Love birds done in
purple enamel.
$495.00.*
Courtesy of Ira Scheck.

*Blue enamel flowers with pearls
and blue pistils/stamens. $395.00.*
Courtesy of Ira Scheck.

*Upright flowers, ruby
rhinestone accents. Dark green
enameled leaves. $595.00.*
Couresty of Ira Sheck.

*Calla lilies.
$350.00.*

*Openfaced
blossoms. $285.00.*

Diamenté American Beauty roses. $595.00.
Courtesy of Ira Scheck.

Left: openfaced blossoms, outer petals with blue enamel, inner petals with diamenté rhinestones. $250.00. Right: pink bell flowers. $595.00.
Courtesy of Ira Scheck.

Gold-plated owls. $195.00.

Diamenté rhinestones,
Art Deco. $195.00.

Quivering Camellia.
$625.00.

Lucky horseshoe
horses. $595.00.
Courtesy of Ira Scheck.

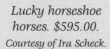

*Ruby-eared, blue-eyed
twin horses.*

Matching earrings.

❧ *Set, $425.00.* ❧

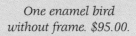

*One enamel bird
without frame. $95.00.*

*Twin pansies without
frame. $85.00.*

Twin bees without frame. $75.00.

Pair of diamenté brooches.
No frame. $65.00.

Blue enamel flowers.
No frame. $70.00.

Single purple enamel flower. $40.00.

One clam. $30.00.

Lonely owl. $30.00.

FRANCOIS

Francois was the birth at Coro of a new concept for a jewelry line. Always in the 32 years Coro had been in business, all jewelry had the trademark of the company. Now it was the 1930s, and times were "a changin'."

Coro felt it necessary to create a totally new marketing approach. Research indicated that the fashion world was enamored with Art Deco. Geometric lines were being repeated in furniture, clothes, architecture, almost everywhere.

The Paris Exposition Internationale des Arts Docratifs et Industriales Modernes of 1925 had fired the Art Deco movement. But if French-inspired geometric lines were used in a jewelry line, shouldn't the jewelry be given a French name? Legend has it that Francois was a real-life designer, but Coro's alumni say this is just a fable. *Francois* was just one of many French names suggested.

A special campaign had been done for Bloomingdale's of New York in 1938. The store wanted an exclusive line for its discerning customers. Coro came up woth the name of a fictitious French designer, Francois. Francois was featured in promotional advertising.

The new name fit so well the company decided to take an entirely new step and actually mark the jewelry with the marketing line name. For the first time, Coro produced jewelry marked with another logo.

Francois jewelry would be marketing as an "in-case" line and sold only in the finer stores. It was the first couturier line developed by Coro and reigned supreme as an in-case line.

Francois, 1961.

❧ Logos as they would appear on the back of jewelry. Year of use is indicated whenever possible.❧

Deep pink double-petal blossom. Brooch has black enamel stem with green leaves. $98.00.

White enamel, double-petal staggered blossom, black stem with green leaves.

Matching earrings.

❧ *Set, $125.00.* ❧

White enamel lily has enameled black stem and green leaves. $95.00.

*Light and dark blue
rhinestone fruit brooch. $68.00.*

Cameo. $90.00.

Matching earrings.

*Gold-plated, long-stemmed rose bud,
with pink navettes edged with
diamenté rhinestones.*

❧ Set, $225.00. ❧

*Green enamel leaves,
chalcedony stones.
$98.00.*

*Pair of crown earrings.
Red and green
cabochons. $80.00.*

VENDÔME

As beads are strung one by one, so Coro's top-of-the-line division came into being one step at a time. Vendôme had been a very familiar name to generations of Parisians, for it was the name of the street in Paris, France, where the couturier houses were located, houses that had dressed the most fashionable, famous women from all over the world for decades. Vendôme was a name that brought visions of exquisite costumes to mind. And, of course, a best-dressed woman must complete her outfit with jewelry before she goes out in public.

It is no wonder that this famous street name was suggested by a female Coro worker, Richtie Gady, as a name for a new line in 1944. This was going to be a line based on French fashions, and the name won the vote of the committee. Gady's forte was naming the new Coro lines, and she was noted for her ability to pick just the right one. There was a stock number required for each item, but the salesmen sold items by names, so names were very important.

World War II had ended. The entire world was celebrating, and women were once again anxious to dress up for their men, who were returning from the battlefields. Coco Chanel had paved the way, making it fashionable for Parisian women to wear costume jewelry, sometimes mixed with precious metal pieces. Now Coro wanted to create a high French fashion couturier jewelry.

MIKE TANCER

As an acknowledgement of the power of the French influence, Gerald Rosenberg, president of Coro, baptized the line "Vendôme." The goal was to create a quality jewelry line in a limited quantity, to replace the Art Deco look of Francois. Vendôme was a "bead house" specializing in necklace and earring sets that reflected the artistry of the head designer, Helen Marion.

Mr. Rosenberger had the concept of putting the in-case line as well as the top-of-the-case line in jewelry department stores. The new product was not going to be on top of the glass jewelry store display cases with the inexpensive pieces. No, instead it would be enthroned inside the case with the expensive fine pieces. It was a Lord & Taylor–type of product rather than a Gimbel's or Macy's item.

Coro selected Mike Tancer as the first president of Vendôme. At that period of time, there were three divisions of the company (Coro, Corocraft, and Vendôme) that were run independently, with competitive rivalry.

At one period of time, a six-foot-high wall was erected between Coro and Vendôme workers, to be sure that the divisions were securely working in their own departments without any hint of piracy. There was never the approach taken that if a piece of jewelry was successful, Coro would make a less expensive version for the Coro line.

Vendôme pearls became the meat and potatoes of the business; that was where the money was being made. Those were the days when no woman would consider going out without a strand of pearls around her neck. Richleiu was very, very big in the late 1950s, and Coro was after that part of the market. The Vargo pearls became very popular. They were similar to a string of ordinary pearls with a fancy clasp, but the pearls were elliptical in shape. Collectors should be on the watch for these strands, as they have a great deal of value. Vargo pearls became a hot item, competing with Richleiu pearls in boutique and jewelry departments.

DON STEVENS

And now we begin the second strand of our beaded necklace, with the arrival on the Vendôme scene of Don Stevens. Where did he fit in? Let's begin in 1919, with the arrival in the United States of an 18-year-old Armenian immigrant named Yvette Sahakian. He decided to Americanize his name, as many choose to do during that time. Recalling that a hotel where he spent enjoyable time in Paris was called the Stevens, he took the name as a good luck charm, and took the first name of Erwin. He settled down, got married, became the proprietor of a grocery store, and the family was enriched with the arrival of a son.

Young Donald was surrounded by his father's brothers, who had chosen the jewelry industry as their trade. It was very simple in those days; people could go into the jewelry industry anytime they wanted, they just needed the desire. One uncle was making ear wires in a cottage industry, that is, an industry in which the work was done at home by the family. Soon, eight-year-old Don was making ear wines on the family's kitchen table, his first venture in the career field that was to last all his life. Another uncle, Henry Sahakian, owned NarMar (named after his own daughters, *Nancy* and *Marie*) and made jewelry for Albert Weiss.

Don went on to the University of Rhode Island, graduating in 1953, and was drafted immediately for the Korean War. According to Mr. Stevens, he got out of the service in 1955 with "all sorts of money in my pocket that I had never had before, and I decided to see the world," and he traveled until February 1956. That was the month that Mr. Stevens gave young Don an ultimatum to get a job or get out of the house.

In February 1956, with his father's strong encouragement, Don went to Coro and enrolled in the unofficial jewelry college of Rhode Island by taking a $1.00 an hour job. He was the only college graduate working there. The news got out, and immediately supervisors began giving the young man more complicated assignments.

Adolph Katz realized the potential of Stevens and further his career; before long, the man with the name of a Parisian hotel was the president of the line inspired by Parisian culture, Vendôme. (See how easily the beads of history are strung?)

Stevens was fortunate to have a super designer, Helen Marion, who oversaw the designing of the jewelry concepts. She lived in New Jersey and would travel to Providence every Monday afternoon and go home every Thursday afternoon. She was able to create miracles in just a three-day workweek.

Her bold hand and brilliantly colored pieces succeeded in pushing sales past Corocraft. Why, she even took cotton balls and had them gilded to be strung as beads on necklaces. There were eight to ten women who did the actual stringing of the beads. The balls proved so popular that the work was distributed to workers in Harlem, then to China, and finally to craftsmen in the Bahamas.

Mr. Stevens relates that he was the overseer of the whole thing, putting it all together and making it happen. He would put the lines together and take a trip around the country. He visited the various parts of the country twice a year.

When pearls lost their popularity, Vendôme brought out a line of enamel goods called Japonica, by designer Florence Marr. The Japonica line was produced by outside vendors. Gene Verri, head designer for Coro, was very instrumental in the creation of non-beaded Vendôme products. Jack Feibelman was involved in creating beaded products.

There was one major market line created around ladies' wristwatches. They did not sell well, so the collection was very short lived.

A Providence resident patented an invention of an adjustable ring with a square-shaped shank. Vendôme bought the patent and produced the only square rings that achieved popularity; these were the most comfortable costume jewelry rings around. Stores did not have to bother with sizes, so limited space in their displays could offer large assortments of styles that would fit any woman. Women were amazed at how a square ring was could fit a round finger; once they tried one on, they were convinced.

Many products were brought in from outside vendors, wholesale manufacturers, to make it possible to extend the lines to a wide range of styles and perhaps coax American women to experiment beyond the basic pearl accessory. Uncle Henry Sahakian found that one of his best customers was that little nephew he taught how to bend ear wires. Alfeo Verrecchia, Gene's brother, was one of the major outside sources, working at Gene's Gem-Craft Company. Best Plastics, owned by Jack Feibelman, was contracted for plastic beads and other findings.

Mike Tancer was in New York and Fritzi Jaffe was in charge of sales. Fritzi handled all the contracts with the major department stores. Vendôme was worn by discerning women until 1970, when the division was closed down and the name sold.

Today's collectors have rediscovered the elegance of Vendôme and are treasuring the fine pieces. The name *Vendôme* still proudly resounds, bring to mind images of French flair and fashion.

POSTSCRIPT

Don Stevens went on to work for Jewel Company of American. Although not generally known for over five years, the Swarovski family was the overseas owner.

Larry Metcalf (Coro Canada) and Don Stevens put together a program. Metcalf temporarily took up residency in the United States as the two men combined their Coro expertise to put together a concept to bring Swarovski into jewelry manufacturing. When the Swarovski family started the business, the company had not had an entry into the United States.

The Swarovski company was the main supplier of rhinestones from Austria. Its employees really did not know the world. Stevens had done a lot of Vendôme business with them and had established a nice working relationship with the Austrian company. Stevens would become a mentor to those at the company.

Don Stevens became the president of Swarvoski USA in late 1976. It then began doing business for Avon. The creation of drop shop type work where the company could gain expertise and train people was planned as the first stage of its business expansion.

The factory was built in 1980. The Swarovski line was an exclusive line sold by stores like Nordstroms. Production was full scale with the Savy line, and then Renel was produced for smaller department stores. In 1990, Stevens took early retirement and the Swarovski family took over company leadership.

"…Vendome by Coro," 1953.

Vendôme Orientale.

Vendôme

⮾ Logo as it would appear on the back of jewelry.
Year of use is indicated whenever possible. ⮾

Triple-strand necklace of faux pearls,
crystal, and gold-tone beads.

⮾ Complete parure, $105.00. ⮾

Triple-strand bracelet and screw-back
earrings complete this parure.

151

*Jewel Manufacturing Co. made the
chain for this convertible parure in the
mid-1970s. Blue baguette necklace.*

*Snowflake brooch can be worn
separately or pinned onto the necklace.
Pattern is repeated in earrings.*

❧ Complete parure, $195.00. ❧

Double-strand pink cabochon necklace.

Matching earrings.

❧ Complete parure, $295.00. ❧

Double-strand bracelet finishes this three-piece parure.

Fall parure starts with orange, green, gold,
and aurora borealis rhinestone earrings.

A five row bracelet
comes next.

A heart-shaped brooch is
the third piece.

The five row pattern repeats
in necklace, the fourth piece
in this grand parure.

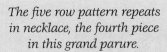

❧ *Grand parure, $895.00.* ❧

Double-strand yellow taffy ball necklace.

The balls are seen again in this three-strand bracelet.

Matching earrings complete this parure.

❧ *Complete parure, $295.00.* ❧

Pearl and silver metallic navette necklace.

Matching bracelet.

The earrings make a
three-piece parure.

❦ Three-piece parure, $245.00. ❧

*Aurora borealis pink necklace
has faceted, large domed
chatons and pink crystal drops.*

*Matching brooch
and earrings.*

❦ *Three-piece parure, $655.00.* ❧

*Carved fruit salad flat backs are featured
on necklace and earrings. Set, $105.00.*

Frosted large bead and small pink crystal necklace with earrings. $105.00.

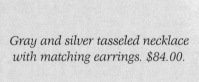

Gray and silver tasseled necklace with matching earrings. $84.00.

Enameled birdcage necklace designed by Florence Marr.

Matching earrings.

❧ Set, $48.00. ❧

*Necklace with pink crystals,
pink beads, and aurora
borealis beads that have green
and pink enamel caps.*

*Matching
earrings.*

❧ *Set, $50.00.* ❧

*Double-strand marbleized and
plain pink bead necklace.*

*Matching
beads.*

❧ *Set, $60.00.* ❧

*Black and gold necklace,
double strand, with
matching screw-back
earrings. Set, $55.00.*

*Beaded necklace, in four shades of
red. Double strand, with matching
earrings. $95.00.*

*Aurora borealis and
milk bead necklace.*

Matching earrings.

❧ Set, $68.00. ❧

Triple-strand clear and gold bead necklace.

Matching earrings

✎ *Set, $65.00.* ✎

Montana gold-wired, blue crystal bead necklace.

✎ *Set, $95.00.* ✎

Matching earrings.

Gold-plated necklace and matching earrings in original gift box. $100.00.

Matching earrings.

❧ Set, $110.00. ❧

Gift box necklace imported from Japan.

Double-strand blue necklace with matching earrings. Set, $85.00 .

Japanned multicolored chaton and pear-shaped rhinestone necklace with six small drops and a large center drop.

Matching clip-back earrings.

Set, $110.00.

*Emerald green
bead necklace.*

*Matching
screw-back
earrings.*

❧ Set, $110.00. ❧

*Frosted bead necklace with
earrings. Set, $85.00.*

*Blue metallic
cabochon necklace.*

Matching earrings.

❧ *Set, $105.00.* ❧

*Yellow, olivine, gold, and pearl beaded
necklace, with full double strand and
two short strands added for full body.*

Matching earrings.

❧ *Set, $95.00.* ❧

*Opera-length gold
necklace with double
chain links. $35.00.*

*Novelty bead necklace
in amber tones.
$38.00.*

Pearls. $50.00.

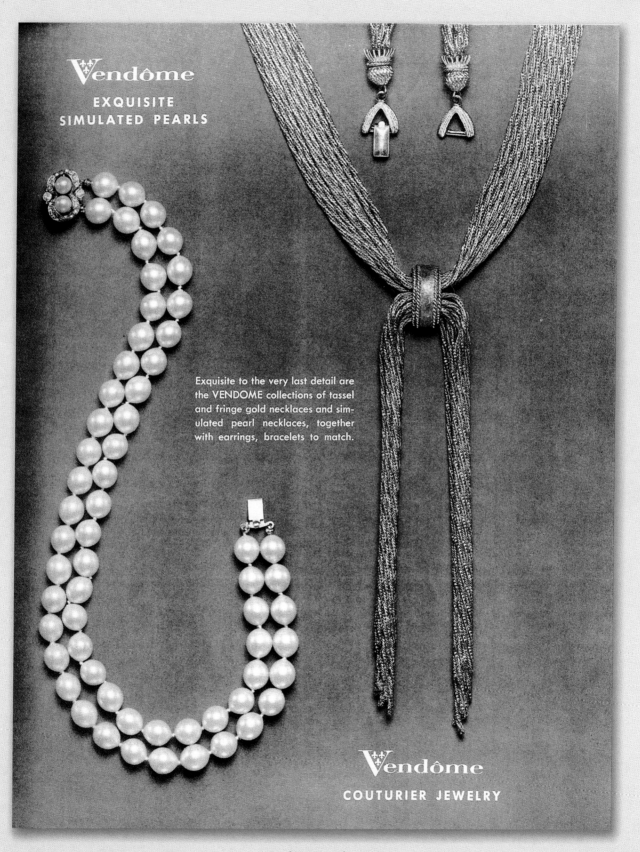

Vendôme Pearls, 1961.

*Silver tube necklace with
removable blue chaton
pendant. $145.00.*

*Golden pendant with large
and small diamenté
chatons. $45.00.*

*Double-strand cranberry
bead and aurora borealis
necklace. $68.00.*

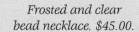

*Frosted and clear
bead necklace. $45.00.*

*Five-strand necklace with
aurora borealis and blue
and black beads. $70.00.*

*Silver chain, filigree
pendant with blue
background. $40.00.*

*Golden necklace with
metallic beads and gold
tassels. $110.00.*

Tiny yellow beads cover each foam ball imported from Japan, and green plastic leaves add a touch of contrast on necklace. $48.00.

Triple-strand faux cherry amber necklace. $85.00.

Five-strand necklace has black and gold beads with chalk and marble large beads. $54.00.

Double-strand necklace with brown beads. $48.00.

Twelve-strand brown tube and clear bead necklace. $55.00.

Green-topped white chalk bead and faux pearl necklace. $45.00.

Aurora borealis beads on this necklace reflect light changing colors at different angles. $40.00.

Butterscotch gift box (imported from Japan) and plain bead necklace. $50.00.

*Frosted bead cluster
necklace. $50.00.*

Chalk white urban bead necklace. $45.00.

*Purple satin-coated foam bead,
double-strand necklace. $48.00.*

*Netted bead necklace.
$45.00.*

Rope with crystal beads. $50.00.

Necklace with one strand of crystal beads and a second strand of clear and blue beads. $50.00.

Faux pearl and black bead necklace. $245.00.

Aurora borealis, pink, and blue rhinestone brooch with earrings. Set, $68.00.

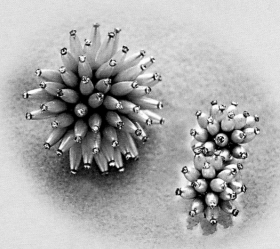

Brooch with an explosion of yellow beads. Matching earings. Set, $55.00.

Brooch and earrings with blue aurora borealis novelty glass blossoms. Set, $55.00.

*Japanned brooch with
clear navettes. Matching
earrings. Set, $75.00.*

*Faux pearl, diamenté
rhinestone brooch. With
earrings. Set, $55.00.*

*Frosted blossom brooch with pastel
green crystal leaves. Matching
earrings. Set, $85.00.*

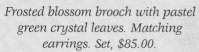

Brooch is an explosion
of frosted beads.
Matching earrings.
Set, $60.00.

Two-toned blue flower
brooch with enamel leaves
and matching earrings.
Set, $105.00.

Three-layer faux pearl,
gold-plated brooch with
earrings. $85.00.

Gold-plated petal, faux pearl and sapphire brooch.

Matching half-blossom earrings.

❧ *Set, $155.00.* ❧

Brooch and earrings with plastic green leaves and orange berries. Tiny orange beads engulf each foam ball. Set, $65.00.

*Brooch with swirl of leaves
and emerald navettes
surrounded by diamenté.*

&⤨ *Set, $140.00.* ⤨&

*Matching
earrings.*

*Brooch with enameled red
petals and faux pearl center.*

*Matching half-
blossom earrings.*

&⤨ *Set, $125.00.* ⤨&

Brooch with translucent long-stemmed blossom with trembler pistil/stamen. Matching earrings. Set, $130.00.

Art Deco dark brown three-corner faceted crystal center with diamenté decorations of many shapes. With matching earrings. Set, $195.00.

❧ *Set, $150.00.* ☙

Emeral green rhinestone set in openwork wings of butterfly.

Matching earrings.

*Brooch with enamel leaves
and black berries.*

Matching earrings.

❧ *Set, $205.00.* ❧

*Aurora borealis blue
blossom brooch.*

*Matching
earrings.*

❧ *Set, $75.00.* ❧

*Brooch with blue crystal petals
that have dark blue tips.*

*Matching
earrings.*

❧   *Set, $80.00.*   ❧

Novelty blue leaf brooch.

Matching earrings.

❧   *Set, $95.00.*   ❧

*Japanned pink rhinestone brooch with
matching earrings. Set, $160.00.*

*Enamel orange blossom brooch with
earrings. Set, $125.00.*

Gene Verri–designed chrysanthemum brooch.

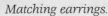

Matching earrings.

❧ *Set, $225.00.* ❧

Matching earrings.

Faux pearl, light and dark blue and diamenté rhinestone brooch with three golden buds.

❧ *Set, $275.00.* ❧

*Golden swirl and crystal
Duette. $195.00.*

*Brooch with faceted, large purple
crystal centers, emerald-cut faux
aquamarine, and different shades
of blue rhinestones. $395.00.*

*Gold-tone, four-leaf, seed
pearl brooch. $65.00.*

*Gene Verri gold-plated prancing unicorn brooch
with faux turquoise and ruby. $125.00.*

Gene Verri griffin. $145.00.

*Gene Verri
crouching lion.
$145.00.*

*Gene Verri
running elephant.
$175.00.*

Pink crystal, gold-plated angel. $95.00.

Gold-plated seahorse. $95.00.

Enameled hummingbird with trembler wings. $165.00.

Enameled tropical bird. $90.00.

*Enameled toucan,
Gene Verri design.
$110.00.*

*Haskell-style
brooch. $70.00.*

*Black and aurora borealis
crystal brooch.*

*Matching
earrings.*

Set, $95.00.

*Crystal rhinestone
rosette brooch.
$70.00.*

*Brooch with plastic
blossoms and rhinestone
center. $95.00.*

*Double-bloom
brooch. $80.00.*

*Crystal tube
bow. $85.00.*

Moonstone and pink and aurora borealis rhinestone brooch. $90.00.

Brooch with green, blue, and black beads, and crystals. $80.00.

White enamel camellia brooch. $95.00.

White and pink enamel blossom brooch. $75.00.

*Fruit, apple and pear,
with bites out of each.
Pair, $150.00.*

*Brooch with lavender crystal
blooms, pink blown glass
buds, and enamel leaves.
$135.00.*

*Brooch with gold-
plated wire stems
and yellow enamel
blossom. $110.00.*

Brooch with faux turquoise bead flower and enamel openwork petal. $95.00.

Green crystal bead and emerald green rhinestone brooch. $95.00.

Blue cabochon, silver leaf, blue navette brooch. $85.00.

Black-banded crystal brooch. $110.00.

Another great honor was awarded to Coro in 1938, when the company was selected to produce the commemorative jewelry for the 1938 Friendship Conference of North and South America. The event was to be held in Lima, Peru.

The United States of America was a proud and dedicated member of the organization. First Lady Elenor Roosevelt sponsored a fund drive with the cooperation of the *Ladies Home Journal*. It was the magazine's idea to have an American firm produce a piece of costume jewelry to publicize the event.

Well-known designer Lester Gaba created this memorial. In 1942, the *Amigos Siempre* (Friends Forever) brooch was offered to the general public for $3.95. The royalty proceeds would go directly to the Inter-American Scholarship Fund.

No record has been found of the dollars this flagged brooch generated for the fund. Mrs. Roosevelt would be amazed to know that this friendship brooch is now valued at $1,000 – $1,250 by today's costume jewelry collectors.

Amigos Siempre, $450.00.

Gene Verri dragonfly with enamel wings. $110.00.

Fur clips with faceted ruby red glass centers. Pair, $135.00.

Snowflake brooch with blue rhinestones in different shades. $78.00.

Gold-plated flower.
$78.00.

Novelty crystal blossom brooch. $85.00.

Brooch with chalk white navettes
and enameled leaves accented by
topaz rhinestones. $95.00.

Enameled butterly. $80.00.

Flower brooch with gold-plated
skeleton petals. $85.00.

Pink enamel blossom. $65.00.

Yellow multipetal blossom. $78.00.

Enamel bow. $78.00.

Black rhinestone bow with articulated streamers and edged with diamenté baguettes. $225.00.

Brooch with red rhinestone center and rays of red and white rhinestones. $65.00.

Sophisticated black brooch. $175.00.

Brooch with diamenté navettes that partially cover an emerald green large-faceted crystal. $350.00.

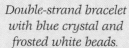

Double-strand bracelet with blue crystal and frosted white beads.

Matching earrings.

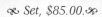

Set, $85.00.

Watch with enameled links. $110.00.

Watch with Art Deco influence. $145.00.

Ring, dark purple with gold-plated ribs. $55.00.

Ring, domed and studded with cabochons. $45.00.

Square-shank ring. $55.00.

Ring with green emerald center stone. $55.00.

Dome ring with, multicolored cabochons. Side view below left. $55.00.

Emerald-cut crystal ring. Side view below left. $70.00.

Please note the square ring shank.

Aurora borealis earrings. $35.00.

Vendôme Royal Empire.

Pear and gray bead, pink crystal earrings. $30.00.

Black crystal and diamenté rhinestone earrings. $35.00.

Verite blue and diamenté rhinestone earrings. $40.00.

Earrings with navette crystals and dark red rhinestones. $45.00.

Cluster earrings with olivine crystal beads shading to dark blue beads. $45.00.

Gold and silver twisted braid earrings. $25.00.

Mabé pearl barrel earrings with aurora borealis crystal beads. $45.00.

Pearl, gold-plated, diamenté-studded earrings. $40.00.

*Black drop
earrings. $55.00.*

*Red berry, dark blue
drop earrings. $40.00.*

*Blue baguette and chaton
shoulder-duster drop
earrings. $85.00.*

*Pink frosted stone and
crystal bead earrings.
$38.00.*

Gold-plated, diamenté rhinestone earrings. $45.00.

Filigree, green rhinestone earrings. $55.00.

Watermelon crystal earrings rimmed with pink plastic. $65.00.

Crystal and amber bead earrings with diamenté rosettes. $55.00.

THE GOLDEN GIFT OF VENDOME VERMEIL

Genuine sterling silver dipped in a golden bath.
A dazzling contemporary collection of necklaces, bracelets, pins and earrings
suffused with the romance surrounding those treasures famed
throughout history as royal presentations.
Some are jeweled with real ruby chips or with fabulous simulated pearls.
All in magnificent French blue, velvet-lined gift boxes.
Rich, elegant, extravagant in spirit, Vendome Vermeil makes a truly distinguished gift.
Large bow pin, $15.00, ruby chip earrings, $10.00, bracelet, $20.00.

"The Golden Gift of Vendome Vermeil," 1961.

COROCRAFT

The year was 1933, and Coro was considering expanding internationally and entering the European jewelry commerce. A fully operational manufacturing plant was being proposed for the Sussex area, but a legal battle had to be fought first.

The English firm of Ciro objected to the name of *Coro*, because it so closely resembled Ciro's trademark, well established in Europe. Would Coro infringe upon Ciro's business and take over its clientele? This was a highly debated legal discussion that could take years to resolve going through the English courts.

"CHAMBORD" *by Coro*

The elegance of fashionable Paris captured in this smartly styled jewelry by CORO. At all leading stores or write Coro, Inc., New York 1.

Corocraft ®

AMERICA'S BEST DRESSED WOMEN WEAR CORO JEWELRY

© 1953 Coro, Inc., Design Pat. Pend. U.S. Pat. Off.   Prices plus tax.   Write for "Your Coroscope", a FREE booklet containing helpful jewelry hints.

AS SEEN IN HARPER'S BAZAAR MAGAZINE
and TOWN & COUNTRY Magazine

about $25
about $7.50
about $18
about $20

Corocraft Chambord, 1953.

Coro decided to mark all jewelry made at the Sussex plant "Corocraft." It would produce jewelry in the $10 to $50 range. This high-end jewelry included many pieces done in sterling, made by the casting method. (Sterling silver is 92.5% pure silver with 7.5% copper added). The silver was finished with a spray coating of gold wash on either yellow or pink tone gold-plated silver such as this is called vermeil.

The trendy, fashionable pieces feature Art Deco (geometric form) and Art Nouveau (flowing, poetic interpretations of nature) designs. The large plant was fully equipped to handle all stages of manufacturing, but it was dependent on Providence Coro operation for the master molds.

Alfred Katz commanded control of the designs for this line. Gene Verri was the head designer for Corocraft and was mainly responsible for its jewelry. This was an amusing twist of fate that has confused many jewelry collectors. Although the Corocra plant was indeed in England, control of the master molds was held in Providence. Thus, not all Corocraft comes from the English plant, and since the master molds were in Rhode Island, they were used stateside also. The fact does remain that Corocraft was designed for the English market.

Plant markings were not placed on the production pieces, but the quality and perfection of design are very evident in all jewelry bearing the logo. From 1933 until the 1970s, Corocraft was the top line for Coro.

Swarovski bought the Coro operation in England with the intention of using the Coro name to enter the European jewelry industry. Its plans did not work out despite its struggling efforts, and the plant was silenced.

Corocraft Empire, 1954.

Logos as they would appear on the back of jewelry. Year of use indicated when possible.

1935.

1942.

1943.

1944.

Coro Craft (in box)

1940.

1956.

Corocraft

Forget-Me-Not Corocraft.

*Verite ruby red
baguettes highlight
ribbon bow from 1961.*

*Matching
earrings.*

❧ *Set, $135.00.* ❧

*Red chaton and
diamenté baguette
striped heart.*

*Matching clip
earrings.*

❧ *Set, $150.00.* ❧

*Gold-plated brooch with
diamenté blossom drop.*

❧ *Set, $85.00.* ❧

*Matching
clip earrings.*

*Row of green rhinestones and row
of orange rhinestone frame large
dark green crystal in brooch.*

Matching earrings.

❧ *Set, $175.00.* ❧

*Blue and green
enamel blossom
brooches.*

*Matching
earrings.*

❧ *Set, $85.00.* ❧

*Art Deco
Christmas tree.*

*Matching
earrings.*

❧ *Set, $85.00.* ❧

Pair of large-mouthed fish, sterling vermeil with enamel fins. Pair, $160.00.

Lucite-bellied fish with blue enamel fins, tail, and head. $395.00.

Golden bird of paradis with red and diamenté rhinestone tail feathers. $175.00.

Hollow sterling rooster. $165.00.

Twin flower retro brooch. $140.00.

Golden fly with green crystal body. $395.00.

Sterling silver Art Nouveau flower. $110.00.

Battle axe and helmet. $225.00.

Sterling brooch with sky blue chatons. $110.00.

Sterling brooch with two flowers and three leaves. $80.00.

Sterling vermeil with faux turquoise. $165.00.

Woven diamenté and red baguette wreath. $90.00.

*Amber and topaz
gold-toned brooch.
$80.00.*

*Golden sunflower with
blue and green
rhinestone center.
$75.00.*

*Multicolored apple
brooch. $95.00.*

*Tucan with colored belly and
enamel tail feathers. Gene
Verri design. $395.00.*

Royal Narcissus by Corocraft.

Enameled iris brooch. $195.00.

Brooch with brushed gold-plated leaves and emerald green chatons. $245.00.

Brooch with brushed gold-plated leaves, ruby cabochons, and gold-plated grape clusters. $195.00.

Enamel long-billed bird with trembling diamenté head and diamenté feathers. $395.00.

*Enamel painted pansy
brooch. $295.00.*

*Red crystal navette
blossom brooch. $80.00.*

*Pearl-eating enamel lizard
with diamenté rhinestone
stripe. $995.00.*

*Double strawberry
brooch with pink and
red rhinestones. $68.00.*

Sterling vermeil, long-stemmed diamenté beauty. $295.00.

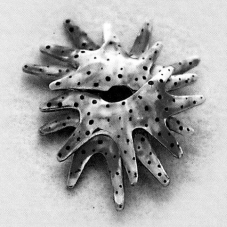

Pink enamel starfish brooch. $75.00.

Pink and green enamel floral brooch. $75.00.

Blue enamel islands on gold-tone circle. $65.00.

Corocraft Jewels for Spring, 1953.

Sterling vermeil, Montana blue navette rhinestone brooch. $110.00.

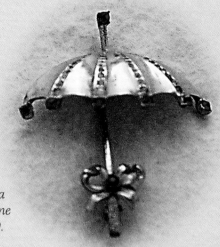

Sterling umbrella with red rhinestone accents. $135.00.

Sterling vermeil, pink and blue pastel flower brooch. $180.00.

Sterling vermeil brooch with three pink chatons. $110.00.

Sterling vermeil brooch with three yellow chatons. $105.00.

Gold-plated necklace with diamenté yellow ribs. $150.00.

Art Deco, japanned necklace with amethyst crystals. $175.00.

Silver necklace with grape cluster that has diamenté navettes. $98.00.

Sterling vermeil five-link bracelet with multicolored rhinestones. $95.00.

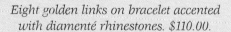

Eight golden links on bracelet accented with diamenté rhinestones. $110.00.

Corocraft Diadem Jewels.

MYLU/TANCER & II

Once upon a time there were two very close sisters, Marge and Lynne. Each grew up, got married, and had children. The devoted sisters were separated by distance, a fact that was the subject of major discussions.

Marge Borofsky and Lynne Gordon had long talks about many things. One frequently discussed subject was, "Why not go into business together?" They spent many hours trying to figure out a way to be close to each other and earn extra Christmas money at the same time.

What would they do, what product could they offer? Shopping together, they spotted holiday corsages, and they immediately knew what they were going to do. They created Christmas corsages nestled in tree shaped boxes. The white bottom of the box was covered by a see-through plastic top.

Since Marge lived in Massachusetts, she took her samples to a Boston store. New Yorker Lynne took her samples to New York City and visited Gimbles. The sisters met with instant success, and the Mylu Design Company was in business. Marge and Lynne were hard put to hand make enough corsages to keep up with the demand. They needed to go to faster production. The two sisters put their heads together and decided to make Christmas jewelry instead. It would be made in Massachusetts and shipped to the New York market.

It wasn't long before they were making Christmas angels, wreaths, deer, and trees and applied for copyrights to their designs. Lynne became the New York salesman and Marge shipped products from Greenfield, Massachusetts. Soon their Christmas items became fast sellers at Filene's, Gimbles, and Penney's, and in the Montgomery Wards catalogs.

Mylu was in business for almost five years, acquiring a good reputation and establishing a fine clinentele base. Perhaps it could be called a compliment that Coro produced some copies of their designs and had them for sale in stores and in advertisements.

Undaunted, the two sisters went to Coro to protest the copyright infringement. Coro president Mike Tancer immediately called to have production stopped and the retail items pulled back from inventory. Acknowledging the standing of the Mylu Christmas line, Mr. Tancer invited the ladies to come aboard Coro.

Flattered by the invitation, the ladies said, "Not at this time, but we'll keep it in mind." In 1968, they accepted his offer, and Mylu became a division of Coro under the presidency of Mike Tancer.

Mylu became responsibile for Coro's Christmas and children's jewelry. Holiday jewelry gifts for Valentine's Day, Mother's Day, and Easter kept the division busy. The sisters stayed on with Coro after Richton took over the company.

In 1970, Chapter 11 closed the Coro doors. The ladies joined Mike Tancer to form Tancer & II. Lynne stayed on for almost nine years before the doors were closed at Tancer & II.

Marge went to Avante (in North Bergen, NJ) and went on to become the vice president. In 1997, she joined K&M Associates, a fashion jewelry merchandise firm. She designed jewelry for the J. C. Penney catalogs and many other firms.

Not bad for two sisters who wanted to earn some extra Christmas money. Never underestimate the power of a woman, or two sisters.

©MYLU   *1968.*

1970.   TANCER II©

❧ *Logos as they would appear on the back of jewelry. Year of use is indicated whenever possible.* ❧

*Mouse carrying
rhinestone-decorated
tree. $58.00.*

*Reindeer, antlers decorated with
multicolored crystal beads. $110.00.*

Enamel green holly bow with red rhinestone berries has a mustard seed. $95.00.

Santa hat with mistletoe is enameled, and puppy has a rhinestone collar. $45.00.

Gold-plated, tiered tree with red crystal beads. $65.00.

Gold-plated, layered tree has multicolored rhinestone ornaments. $60.00.

Gold-plated flowers form tree with rhinestone ornaments. $55.00.

Traditional gold-plated tree with rhinestone ornaments.

Matching earrings.

❧ *Set, $85.00.* ❧

Ruby rhinestone–winged angel carrying red poinsettia flower. $65.00.

Angel holding candle lighter. $65.00.

Angel holding poinsettia. $65.00.

Blue flowers decorate angel. $45.00.

Winged angel. $60.00.

Easter bunny. $60.00.

*Gold-plated branch
with red and gold
ornament. $48.00.*

*Tall tree with rhinestone
ornaments. $50.00.*

*Curled braided rope forms tree with
rhinestone ornaments. $60.00.*

*Gold-plated wreath
and bow with
diamenté rhinestone
ornaments. $55.00.*

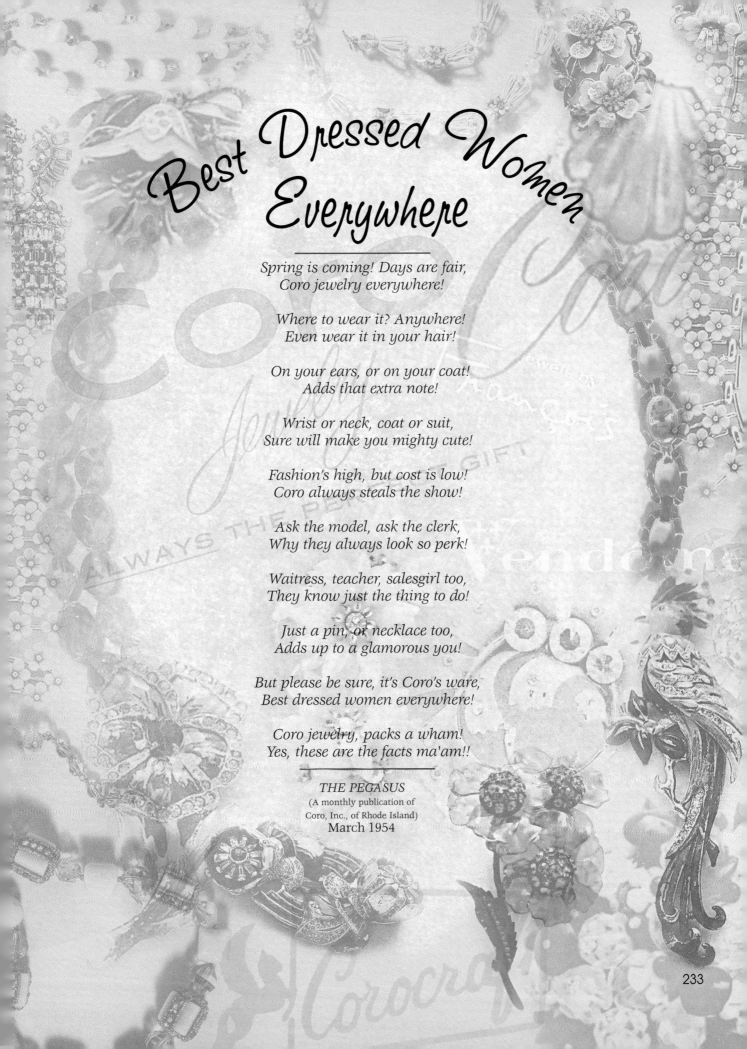

Best Dressed Women Everywhere

Spring is coming! Days are fair,
Coro jewelry everywhere!

Where to wear it? Anywhere!
Even wear it in your hair!

On your ears, or on your coat!
Adds that extra note!

Wrist or neck, coat or suit,
Sure will make you mighty cute!

Fashion's high, but cost is low!
Coro always steals the show!

Ask the model, ask the clerk,
Why they always look so perk!

Waitress, teacher, salesgirl too,
They know just the thing to do!

Just a pin, or necklace too,
Adds up to a glamorous you!

But please be sure, it's Coro's ware,
Best dressed women everywhere!

Coro jewelry, packs a wham!
Yes, these are the facts ma'am!!

THE PEGASUS
(A monthly publication of
Coro, Inc., of Rhode Island)
March 1954

Glossary

Aquamarine — a variety of beryl that is transparent and of various shades of blue and blue-green. Man-made colored light blue glass used in costume jewelry.

Amethyst — a natural gemstone found in shades from lavender to purple. Costume jewelry frequently uses imitation rhinestones in the same shades.

Antique — costume jewelry made before 1950.

Art Deco — style of geometric lines and bold colors. Period of time, 1910 – 1930.

Art Nouveau — designs centered on a poetic interpretation of nature. Period of time, 1890 – 1915.

Articulated — divided into distinct segments that give the piece mobility.

Aurora borealis — microscopic layers of different materials vacuum plated to glass for an iridescent coating. Introduced in 1953.

Baguette — elongated, faceted, straight-sided stones.

Base metal — see **White metal.**

Black diamond — smoky-colored rhinestones. Name given by the Weiss company.

Brass — alloy of copper, tin, and zinc. Dull yellow metal. Earlier antique costume jewelry pieces sometimes used brass as the base metal.

Brooch — a large pin, from the French *broche,* which means "skewer."

Cabochons — non-faceted, rounded, domed stones. Usually flat on underside.

Cartouche — plate bearing company name applied to back of jewelry.

Chatelaine — formerly, long chains fastened at the waist that were hung with the necessary daily items of a housekeeper. Now it is the name for two brooches connected by one or more chains.

Chaton — the most common faceted rhinestone. A cut with 9 to 12 facets, flat tabletop surface, and a bottom that comes to a point.

Citrine — quartz stone ranging from yellow to gold in color. Imitated in rhinestones.

Clipmates — two fur clips on a slide that when complete can be worn as a brooch. Trifari trademark.

Collectibles — costume jewelry manufactured after 1950.

Costume jewelry — jewelry not containing precious jewels or metals.

Couturier — establishment engaged in creating fashionable custom-made women's clothing.

Diamenté — imitation diamonds. Another name for clear rhinestones.

Demi-parure — two matching pieces of the same design. Frequently called a set.

Dentelles — unfoiled, crystal glass, formed in a mold and hand cut. Popular from the 1930s to 1950s.

Dichoric — having the property of presenting different colors in two different directions by transmitted light.

Dress clip — hinged-clasp brooch that can be worn singly or as part of a pair. Inserted on the neckline, a clip can bunch the material together to create a lower neckline.

Duette — two clips mounted on a brooch frame. Made by Coro.

234

Facets — cuts made to shape stones and enhance light refraction.

Faux — French for "false." Used to denote manmade copies of gemstones.

Filigree — open, airy, lacy, decorative metal wire scroll work.

Flat back — used to describe a stone that is flat on the back.

Foil backing — backing applied to rhinestones in a vacuum plating process, using very thin gold or silver metal. This allows light to bounce off the stone and sparkle.

Fur clip — a clip with two long prongs on a steel spring, which allows the decorative clip to be worn on a heavy fabric or fur.

Golden portals — the brass framing around the front doors of the Providence Coro building.

Hallmark — mark on back of jewelry denoting gold or silver content.

Hangtag — removable paper or metal tag bearing company name and attached after production is completed.

In case — costume jewelry valuable enough to be put inside a display case.

Japanned — finished or plated using a black, coal-tar derivative.

Jewelry College — the unofficial name for the Providence Coro plant.

Lacquer — a varnish used to give a smooth finish or appearance.

Lariat — a piece having open ends with drops and a center ornament to hold it together.

Locket — suspended pendant that opens to hold one or more pictures.

Logo — company trademark.

Lucite — acrylic plastic, transparent. DuPont trade name for plexiglass.

Major line — new sample lines shown twice a year.

Marquise — see **Navette**.

Minor line — sample lines with unfavorable items removed and new items added.

Nodder — individual piece mounted on a small spring so it will vibrate when moved.

Opalene — man-made imitation opal.

Openwork — actual design cut into metal, which allows light to filter in.

Opera length — necklaces of lengths that vary from 48" to 90".

Parure — more than two matching pieces of jewelry.

Pavé — stones placed close together, with a minimum of metal showing. Literally "paving over the metal."

Pendant — a drop or design meant to be suspended on a single chain.

Plating — the covering of base metal with a top coat of metal paint.

Pot metal — see **White metal**.

Rhinestone — leaded glass stone with foil backing.

Rhinestone Campus — the name for the Providence building and interiors.

Rhodium — non-tarnishing silver-colored finish. Member of the platinum group of metals.

Set — more than one piece of the same design.

Shoulder duster — drop earring hanging long enough to brush the shoulder of the wearer.

Suite — more than two pieces of the same design; also called a parure.

Sweater guards — two alligator pinch clips chained together. Used to hold sweater front together.

Topaz — gemstone usually ranging in color from yellow to orange.

Trademark — name of specific brand or company.

Trembler — see **Nodder**.

Trunk show — an event at which the salesman shows samples from traveling luggage.

Vacuum plating — process used to foil the backs of rhinestones.

Vermeil — a gold wash over sterling silver. Can have pink or yellow gold finish.

White metal — 92% tin with added cadmium, lead, and zinc. Used to form the first state of costume jewelry. Also called base or pot metal.

Bibliography

Aikens, Ronna Lee. *Brillian Rhinestones*. Paducah, KY: Collector Books, 2003.

Baker, Lillian. *Fifty Years of Collectible Fashion Jewelry 1925 - 1975*. Paducah, KY: Collector Books, 1995.

Ball, Joanne Dubb and Dorothy Hehl Torem. *Costume Jewelers: The Golden Age of Design*. Atglen, PA: Schiffer Publishing Ltd., 1993.

Becker, Vivienne. *Fabulous Costume Jewelry*. Atglen, PA: Schiffer Publishing Ltd.,1993.

Brown, Marcia. "A Diamond Anniversary." *Vintage Fashion & Costume Jewelry*, vol. 2 no. 1, Winter 2001.

Brunalti, Carla and Roberto. *American Costume Jewelry*. Milan, Italy: Gabriele Massotta, 1997.

___. *A Tribute to America*. Milan, Italy: EDITA, 2002.

Cannizzaro, Maria Teresa. *Bijoux American*. Milan, Italy: Federico Motta, 2003.

Cera, Deanna Farretti. *Jewels of Fantasy*. New York, NY: Abrams, 1992.

___. *Amazing Gems*. New York, NY: Harry N. Abrams, Inc., 1997.

Coro. *Coronet*, Coro in-house magazine, 1945.

___. *50th Anniversary History & Sales Manual*, 1951.

___. *The Pegasus*, a Coro monthly publication, March 1954.

Dolan, Maryanne. *Collecting Rhinestone & Colored Jewelry*. Florence, AL: Books Americana, 1990.

Ettinger, Roseanna. *Popular Jewery 1840 – 1940*. Atglen, PA: Schiffer Publishing Ltd., 1990.

___. *Popular Jewelry 40s, 50s*. Atglen, PA: Schiffer Publishing Ltd., 1994.

___. *Popular Jewelry of the 60s, 70s & 80s*. Atglen, PA: Schiffer Publishing Ltd., 1997.

Gallina, Jill. *Christmas Pins, Past & Present*. Paducah, KY: Collector Books. 2004.

Gordon, Angie. *Twentith Century Costume Jewelry*. Carle Place, NY: Adasia International, 1990.

Leshner, Leigh. *Rhinestone Jewelry*. Iola, WI: Krause Publications, 2002.

Leshner, Leigh. *Vintage Jewelry*. Iola, WI: Krause Publications. 2002.

Miller, Harrice Simmons. *Costume Jewelry: Confident Collector*. New York, NY: Avon, 1994.

Miller, Judith. *Collector's Guides Costume Jewelry*. New York, NY: DK Publishing, 2003.

Newman, Harold. *An Illustrated Dictionary of Jewelry*. New York, NY: Thames & Hudson, Inc., 1981.

Parker, Deborah. "Duettes." *Vintage Fashion & Costume Jewelry*, vol. 9 no. 3, Summer 1999.

Rainwater, Dorothy. *American Jewelry Manufacturers*. Atglen, PA: Schiffer Publishing Ltd., 1988.

Rezazadeh, Fred. *Costume Jewelry*. Paducah, KY: Collector Books, 1998.

Salsbery, David and Lee. *ABCs of Costume Jewelry*. Atglen, PA: Schiffer Publishing Ltd., 2003.

Schiffer, Nancy. *The Best of Costume Jewelry*. Atglen, PA: Schiffer Publishing Ltd., 1996.

___. *Costume Jewelry – The Fun of Collecting*. Atglen, PA: Schiffer Publishing Ltd., 1992.

___. *Costume Jewelry – The Great Pretenders*. Atglen, PA: Schiffer Publishing Ltd., 1996.

___. *Rhinestones*. Atglen, PA: Schiffer Publishing Ltd., 1993.

Seal, Pat. "Researching Costume Jewelry." www.illusionjewels.com, 2003.

Shatz, Sheryl Gross. *What's It Made Of*. Santa Ana, CA: Benjamin Shatz, 1992.

Simonds, Cherri. *Collectible Costume Jewelry*. Paducah, KY: Collector Books, 1997.

Tempesta, Lucille. "Coro, Coro, Coro." *Vintage Fashion & Costume Jewelry*, vol. 3 no. 3, Summer 1993.

Tolkein, Tracy and Henrietta Wilkinson. *A Collector's Guide to Costume Jewelry*. Willowdale, CT: Firefly Books, Ltd., 1997.

Trowbridge, Nancy Yunker. *Christmas Tree Pins*. Atglen, PA: Schiffer Publishing Ltd., 2002.

Index

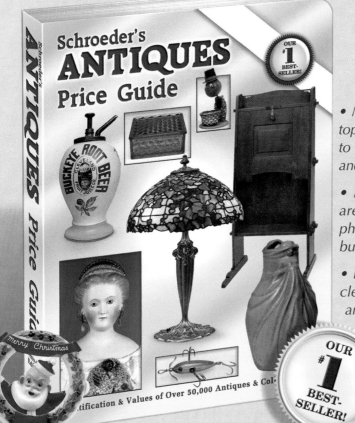